VAMPIRES

Bernhardt J. Hurwood

VAMPIRES

Bernhardt J. Hurwood

quick fox

New York · London

Book design by Nina Clayton
Cover design by Dudley Thomas
Front cover photography by Herbert Wise

International Standard Book Number: 0-8256-3202-1
Library of Congress Catalog Card Number: 80-52713

In Great Britain: Book Sales Ltd., 78 Newman Street, London
    W1P 3LA.
In Canada: Gage Trade Publishing, P.O. Box 5000, 164 Com-
    mander Blvd., Agincourt, Ontario M1S 3C7.

In Memoriam: Laura M. Hurwood 1926-1979

ACKNOWLEDGMENTS

To express my appreciation adequately for all the enthusiastic encouragement and valuable assistance given me during the writing of this book would take an entire chapter. I must particularly cite my editor, Jim Charlton; my agent, Jane W. Wilson; Radu and Nicole Florescu; Dr. Jeanne Youngson, founder of the Count Dracula Fan Club, who opened doors for me and gave of her time and free reign in her personal library; Coco Smith, who put in long, grueling hours assisting me with the bibliography and filmography; Dorothy Nixon and Fern S. Miller of the Vampire Information Exchange; Vincent Mattocks, who contributed his expertise long-distance from England; and other members of the Count Dracula Fan Club who generously gave of their time, notably Freddie Francis and Carol Ann Lombardo. I also wish to thank filmmakers Roy Frumkes and Dr. Carel Rowe, for sharing their expertise in the realm of the cinema. And finally a word of gratitude to my friends and colleagues of the American Society of Journalists and Authors for their moral support—and for being there.

Bernhardt J. Hurwood

CONTENTS

Chapter 1

THE VAMPIRE AND HIS ROOTS

Nowhere in the realm of darkness is there to be found an entity considered more malevolent than the vampire. Since the earliest periods of recorded history vampires have been known to emerge from the shadows to cast a pall of dread as they preyed upon and terrorized their human victims. What has happened then, in the twentieth century, to cause a gradual shift of opinion as to the true nature of the vampire? Certainly there have been ample, well-documented instances in relatively recent times of vampires who have committed the most gruesome and savage depredations on their victims. But can the same thing be said of seemingly ordinary humans categorized as sadistic criminals? Curiously enough, there is a growing trend toward understanding the vampire in modern times. Could it be that vampirologists of earlier days, who flourished in environments of superstition and prejudice, may have inadvertently tipped the scale somewhat unfairly against the vampire?

Vampires, like their human counterparts, have been forced to adapt with the passage of time. No creature, whether it thrives in sunlight or darkness, can avoid extinction unless it evolves. Recent studies have proven conclusively that vampires, particularly in this century, have undergone radical evolutionary changes to allow them to successfully cope with vicissitudes of twentieth-century existence. Later in the book, we will examine many aspects of the vampire's personality, physiology, and habits. In short, we will scrutinize all the known mundane facets of vampirism ordinarily overlooked in most studies. Since we are searching for truth, we will have to ask: What are the myths? What are the realities? What is the origin of the more bizarre superstitions pertaining to the vampire? All these questions and more will be resolved, I hope, in the pages ahead. First let's examine some of the lore of the vampire that has come down to us from the past. Then, from that perspective, we can examine some more recent theories that will shed light on a subject which has drawn and repelled devotees since the earliest of times.

There is no way of knowing with certainty when and how the very first vampires stalked the darkness in search of human blood. We do know that mankind was aware of their existence in ancient times, and judging from the wide variety of legends, superstitions, and true accounts we can state with a reasonable degree of authority that vampires have manifested themselves in a multitude of guises around the world and throughout history. To make an analogy, to say that the only kind of vampire that exists is the familiar figure popularized by Dracula films is like saying that there is only one kind of dog, cat, or bat.

To digress for a moment, let's take a brief look at the bat. Of the nine hundred varieties of bat, most eat fruits, flowers, and insects, although some prey on fish, lizards, and other small creatures. Some are even cannibals. Bats come in all sizes, shapes and colors, ranging from tiny creatures no larger than hummingbirds to fast flying balls of fur with wingspans approaching the five-foot mark. There are dog-faced bats, horse-faced bats, pig-faced bats, big-eared bats, and flying foxes, to mention only a few. Of the sixteen varieties native to the United States, some are ugly and a few are beautiful—like the hoary bats, which belong to the species generally called silver-haired bats. With a coat of rich, soft, luxurious fur, these bats, coming in shades of mahogany and brown tinged with frost, have a sixteen-inch wingspread, making them among the largest of domestic bats. Why then should not vampires come in an infinite number of shapes and varieties?

One of the biggest obstacles in the search for the origin of the vampire is the intense, often acrimonious controversy that has always surrounded the subject. For example, virtually everything written over a hundred years ago represents the extremist viewpoint, regardless of which side it happens to take. Some vampirologists treated the subject as worthy of nothing but contempt, as mere superstition. Others dealt with it from a purely theological point of view and occasionally from a legalistic one. Anthropologists and folklorists in modern times approach vampires from the standpoint of myth. Psychologists regard them as deviates. Occultists, on the other hand, have always adhered to the purely supernatural aspects (for instance, the late Reverend Montague Summers, one of the most prodigious scholars on the subject in the twentieth century, went to his grave vigorously proclaiming that vampires were voracious, blood-sucking, animated corpses). And finally, sensationalists have always gone out of their way to dredge up blood, gore, and horror for its own sake, often overlooking the more subtle aspects of the matter.

The earliest vampire on record was a horribly malefic Assyrian spirit called the Ekimmu. It was not exactly a vampire as we think of them today. It was more of a cross between a ghost and a demon. It did not merely haunt its victims, it often attacked and

Vampiric Nightmare, by Max Klinger.

devoured them. When it was not exercising its voracious appetite, it was believed to possess its victims. So fearsome a demon was the Ekimmu that it was said upon occasion to wipe out entire households merely by appearing within their four walls.

A more recognizable ancient vampire was the Babylonian demon Lilitu. She was either converted or adopted by the ancient Hebrews, who called her Lilith. According to Talmudic legend she was the first wife of Adam, and after refusing to obey him, was banished from the Garden of Eden as punishment. Indeed, she may be the first feminist on record. Thereafter, says the legend, she became a haunter of the darkness, a demon of the night. She struck terror into the hearts of the people by swooping down out of the night to suck the blood of helpless infants and children. She was also held directly accountable for erotic dreams of men, a serious matter indeed, for the loss of semen in this manner was regarded with horror. After the advent of Christianity, early church fathers looked upon her as queen of the night, mistress of the Incubi and Succubi, lewd demons or spirits who assumed human shape and seduced unwilling victims, frequently causing embarrassing pregnancies in the ranks of nuns and virtuous women.

Characteristically similar to Lilith was the Lamia of ancient Greece. She was a demon depicted with the head and breasts of a woman and the scaly body of a winged serpent. Like her predecessor she was a night-flying, bloodsucking monster who preyed primarily on the young. Following in the footsteps of so many other Greek gods and beasts, she was incorporated into the Roman supernatural pantheon as the Strix. The plural of the word Strix in Latin was Strigae, which found its way into Italian as Strega, or witch.

One of the earliest accounts of a phenomenon that could only be interpreted as vampirism in the erotic sense appeared in a book by Phlegon of Tralles, *De Rebus Mirabilis,* or *Of Miraculous Things*, around 125 A.D. The story concerns a young woman named Philinnion and her lover, a young man named Machates. Not long after they fell deeply in love, Philinnion died. Six months after her death she returned bodily from the grave in order to recapture the love-filled nights denied the unhappy pair by her untimely end. Eventually her parents, Demonstratus and Charito, heard about her reappearance and confronted Machates. He was in anguish, for until now he had not known that she was dead. She had told him this in the beginning, but he had assumed that she was a love-starved stranger who resembled his lost sweetheart and had bought the clothing and jewelry from grave robbers.

The next night, Machates secretly dispatched a slave to fetch her mother and father, and when they came they were speechless with joy and amazement at the sight of her, pale and wan, but seemingly alive and well. They threw themselves upon her but she remained cool and distant, saying, "Father and mother, cruel indeed have ye been in that ye grudged my living with the stranger for three days in my father's house, for it brought harm to no one. But ye shall pay for your meddling with sorrow. I must return to the place appointed for me, though I came not hither without the will of heaven." With these words she fell to the floor lifeless, never to move again. Machates, in despair, committed suicide.

What is so fascinating about this strange tale is that it parallels similar complicated love affairs between the living and the dead that can be found in the lore of China and Japan. More specifically, it inspired a long poem by Goethe called *The Bride of Corinth*.

Artist's rendition of Greek Strix *or*
Roman Lamia *attacking her victim.*

In the story a young Christian girl falls in love with a pagan. They are engaged to be married, but she dies. He comes to visit her parents afterward, not knowing of her untimely death. Just as in the Greek account by Phlegon of Tralles, the girl is cold and pale, but makes passionate love to her sweetheart. The mother interrupts them and the girl reproaches her bitterly for her cruelty and pleads that she and her lover be placed in the same tomb together, explaining that by breathing life into her with his tender kisses he has doomed himself to share her fate.

In the next chapter we will delve more deeply into the nether world of vampires in different parts of the world. But first it would be appropriate to raise the question of vampires and their origin, not only from ancient written accounts, but from a scientific point of view. As the nineteenth-century theologian Tryon Edwards said, "Superstitions are for the most part shadows of great truths."

A few years ago a brilliant young British molecular biologist, Dr. David J. Garwes, while conducting genetic research in the United States, became interested in the subject of vampirism and expressed some intriguing theoretical possibilities as to its origin. He suggested that there may have been a connection between vampires and rabies. "The symptoms of rabies," he said, "have about three stages. The first stage is a tingling sensation and soreness, a loss of appetite, restlessness, sleeplessness, melancholia, irritability. This only lasts for about forty-eight hours. But stage two is one of general excitement, furious spasms, difficult breathing and convulsions, and of course, hydrophobia. The sound of someone even speaking about water causes a contraction of the larynx and the victim can't breathe. The sight of water is equally effective."

Could this not be related to the fact that according to vampirologists, vampires could not cross water? Another sign of vampirism frequently mentioned in old accounts was that vampires themselves had ravenous appetites, which caused them to eat their own shrouds, the linings of their coffins, and sometimes even their own fingertips.

Paralleling this, Dr. Garwes described the furious form of rabies in a dog when he "goes around snapping at everybody, biting everything in sight, he will eat anything, too; he will eat straw, he will eat anybody. This isn't because it is a nervous factor. Humans won't try to bite ordinarily, unless they have lost all sense of rationality. To put it simply, they go a bit crazy in the second stage. Their senses are so heightened they might try to eat their pillows."

He went on to make a comment on the concept of vampires metamorphosing into bats. He said, "I don't know if there are any bloodsucking bats in Europe, but the fact that Florida bats can carry rabies makes it a distinct possibility that bats in Europe might have been associated with it. And, as I said before, any rabid animal will bite anything in its path, not for food, but because it has these muscular contractions."

Another aspect of vampirism discussed by Dr. Garwes was a very critical one, namely the fact that vampires, when exhumed from their graves even after having been buried for long periods of time, always appeared to be fresh and lifelike and unaffected by the ravages of decomposition. Dr. Garwes felt there was a definite scientific explanation for this. He said, "I believe for a start that persons who have been poisoned with very strong chemicals tend not to decay because the poison would tend to be equally fatal to the bacteria which cause decay. It reminds me of

Hamlet. In Act V, during the gravedigger's scene, the gravedigger says that a tanner will last nine years because his skin is so tanned by his trade that he won't decay. The water doesn't get in. But I don't know of any disease that will stop normal decay. It would have to be something that stops the bacteria from decomposing the body."

He then went on to say that "the problem these days is that no one can define death. There may be a legal definition, but scientifically, there is no definition of death. What is death? When the heart stops beating? Because if that's the case, then you become reincarnated if they can start it up again by massage. Your nails will continue to grow for months after you have been buried. Hair will continue to grow, because the body is made up of millions of tiny cell units, and just because you have severed control from the brain, which means that you have no control, and perhaps the heart stops beating, doesn't mean that the cells which make up the lining of the stomach, or the skin, or anything else, are actually dead."

Another area that Dr. Garwes covered was the psychology of early times. How many accounts have we read of vampire graves being opened, stakes being driven through the hearts, and blood gushing out as the vampire uttered spine-chilling shrieks of anguish? Said Dr. Garwes, "If only one person was buried alive, and was still alive when the stake was driven through the heart, reports about it would be so exaggerated, they might color all the myths about the entire field, and after all, superstition was tremendous in those days. What would happen in an extremely superstitious community if just a single person was exhumed and a stake driven through the heart, and out came some blood? Not a great gusher, but just a trickle of blood. It would create such an emotional reaction that by the time it had been

repeated a few times, the story would be blown completely out of proportion."

Perhaps one of the most interesting theories offered by Dr. Garwes was that of mutation. In the literature of vampirism there has been a repeated correlation between outbreaks of plague and outbreaks of vampirism. On that Dr. Garwes said, "There is no reason why a disease which may have been prevalent in medieval Europe is no longer known in medicine today. I can't think of any specific cases where this might have occurred, but there is a theory that the Black Death, which hit Europe around the fifteenth century, might have been going around in a mild form for centuries without causing any alarm whatsoever, but that something changed the organism. A mutation arose somewhere along the line that was being transmitted in that very mild, avirulent form, and that this change made it highly pathogenic, and caused endless deaths."

Equally, a civilization might have been hit by a tremendously virulent organism; this organism could have changed so that there is no sign of it today. Thus, it is quite possible that vampirism or lycanthropy (the werewolf syndrome) could have been associated with, not caused by, some disease that disappeared completely from modern civilization. It could have been the common cold or influenza, which have since changed their form. But in those days it might have been a plague that could wipe out a civilization just in the way measles devastated the Fijians.

"In other words, a disease which might have been prevalent long ago throughout Europe could have changed slightly and given rise to very odd effects, and then changed again. Of course, we couldn't possibly have any record of what that was in the first place, so there is no way now of checking into what might have been."

The vampire Carla, played by Ingrid Pitt, emerging from her coffin in the 1970 Amicus-Cinerama film, The House That Dripped Blood, *starring Christopher Lee, Peter Cushing, Nyree Dawn Porter, and Denholm Elliot.*

THE NOSFERAT

The Nosferat not only sucks the blood of sleeping people, but also does mischief as an incubus or succubus. The Nosferat is the stillborn, illegitimate child of two people who are similarly illegitimate. It is hardly put under the earth before it wakes to life and leaves its grave never to return. It visits people by night in the form of a black cat, a black dog, a beetle, a butterfly, or even a simple straw. When its sex is male it visits women; when female, men. With young people it indulges in sexual orgies until they get ill and die of exhaustion. In this case it also appears in the form of a pretty girl or handsome youth, while the victim lies half awake and submits unresistingly. It often happens that women are impregnated by this creature and bear children who can be recognized by their ugliness and by their having hair over the whole body. Then they become witches. . . . The Nosferat appears to bridegrooms and to brides and makes them impotent and sterile.

Heinrich von Wlislacki, quoted
by Ernest Jones in *On the Nightmare*.

Andree Melly (L) and Yvonne Monlaur (R) in The Brides of Dracula, *Hammer Films, 1960.*

Now, to take Dr. Garwes's hypotheses a step or two further, suppose long ago certain mutations occurred in some humans, causing them to become something not quite human, and evolving into a species that subsisted on blood, was noctural in its habits, and was endowed with superhuman strength. Now, if such mutations did indeed appear, they would learn very early that by nature of their very difference they would be feared, hated, and subjected to all manner of persecution. Their natural instinct for self-preservation would undoubtedly cause them to make every effort to survive. Isn't it logical, then, that being endowed with human intelligence they would more than likely employ extraordinary means to ensure that survival? Is it not also logical that it would be to their advantage to create myths concerning their own invincibility, supernatural powers, and general physical superiority? What is more awesome than the ability to conquer death, to exercise absolute power over others, to be free of the bonds imposed upon ordinary mortals by temporal authority? Although no vampire has ever admitted anything about its true nature, there is every reason to believe that what you have just read is closer to the truth than anything ever before suggested.

Assuming that vampires themselves have encouraged and reinforced much of the myth and superstition surrounding them, let's examine some of the strange, and in some cases absurd, beliefs that have sprung up and been perpetuated over the centuries. Without

ORIGIN OF THE WORD VAMPIRE

The word vampire *first came into general English usage some time during the eighteenth century. Some experts maintain that the actual origin of the word stems from the Magyar* vapir. *Other authorities insist that the actual origin of the word is* uber, *a Turkish word meaning witch. Variations in Slavonic tongues are* vampir *in Bulgarian and Serbian,* upier *in Polish, and* upyr *and* vopyr *in Russian. Some assert that there is a relationship with the Lithuanian word* wempti, *meaning to drink.*

Nowhere in the world do we find a vampire more loathsome than the European variety. He is the utter personification of Evil, being dreadful to look upon, malevolent in his behavior, and disgustingly offensive to the sense of smell. Physical descriptions appear frequently in folklore and often they are so ghastly that they tax the imagination. The faces are reported to be pale but lifelike. The eyes when open are glazed and glaring, the lips full and red, drawn back over gleaming, razor-sharp teeth. Often the mouth is said to be found open in a hideous gape, exuding an indescribably fetid stench. Black, ugly clots of blood form stains where it trickled out of the corners and dripped over the chin and onto the clothing. In some instances the coffin itself is depicted as drenched with fresh blood. The vampire is swollen and bloated from its sanguinary feast so that when it is pierced with a stake, or the head is severed, blood gushes forth like a fountain to the accompaniment of frightful shrieks from the corpse.

From Bernhardt J. Hurwood,
The Vampire Papers

doubt some of the bizarre beliefs concerning vampires had a certain basis in fact. For example, in the days before enbalming, premature burial was not an uncommon event. Image the agonies endured by some hapless individual entrapped in the airless confines of the coffin, suffocating in the impenetrable blackness of the grave. Imagine the terror, the despair that would ultimately drive the poor unfortunate to tear at his own flesh, to rip his cerements, to inflict such grievous wounds on himself as to ultimately bleed to death. If a grave containing such a person were to have been exhumed, would it not be logical for superstitious investigators, who were fully expecting to find a vampire, to assume that they had indeed located one?

Take another example, the idea that garlic will ward off vampires. Once again, pure logic will lead to a reasonable explanation. Since vampires have always been associated with death and the grave, and historical records often contain accounts of vampire epidemics during outbreaks of the Black Death, it goes without saying that the noxious stench of decaying flesh would be present. What could be more effective, especially for those too poor to afford precious perfumes and colognes, than to employ some natural means of masking that terrible odor?

There were other superstitions concerning the vampire which were purely religious in origin. For example, it was believed among the Orthodox Greeks that anyone born on Christmas Day was in danger of becoming a vampire. This was a punishment meted out to the mother for having the temerity to give birth on the anniversary of the immaculate conception. Another Greek superstition held that redheaded individuals were potential vampires, for traditionally Judas Iscariot was a redhead. Whereas in the Roman Church an incorrupt body was deemed a sign

of sainthood, quite the opposite view was taken in the Orthodox Church. A popular curse in olden times among the Greeks was, "May the Earth not receive thee!" If the earth did not receive a body, then it would not decay, and the biblical injunction, "Dust to dust," would be unfulfilled. The body would be undead and doomed to stalk the darkness as a vampire.

The most prevalent European belief was that the bite of a vampire turned the victim into a vampire too and thus perpetuated the species. In some areas it was held that individuals who lived an especially depraved life were very likely to become vampires after death. This was the most common factor in the evolution of the Greek vampire or *vrykolakos*. Its habit was to leave the grave at night and go forth to seek victims, frequently knocking on doors and calling victims by name.

A vampire of this type appeared in the twelfth century in the Scottish town of Berwick. According to the chronicler, William of Newburgh, the Berwick vampire was a poor but extremely evil man who began terrorizing the district immediately after his death. Referred to as a dreadful, bloodsucking fiend, he stalked the night with a pack of diabolical, howling dogs. Even those who were not bitten but merely had contact with him became infected with the plague. Eventually ten brave young men were selected by the authorities to deal with the monster. They dug up his grave and burned his corpse to ashes. Unhappily, despite their efforts a terrible outbreak of the plague occurred shortly afterward, killing more people than before.

Since most of these beliefs were rooted in superstition and ignorance, it was only logical for people to believe in even more incredible things, such as the ability of a vampire to metamorphose into a bat, a fly, a black cat, or even a wisp of smoke. Many of these beliefs, it should be noted, were directly related to the idea that witches could fly on broomsticks. The modern expression "fly-by-night" originally referred to the witches' alleged ability to fly, and interestingly enough, many witches of the time firmly believed that they were capable of accomplishing this feat. Incredible as it may seem, there is a perfectly logical explanation for it today when we examine the nature of certain concoctions the witches brewed up and used. Some of the ingredients included opium, belladonna, and rye mold, the latter being a basic element in an LSD-like drug.

Put yourself in the vampire's shoes for a moment: wouldn't it seem logical to take every possible advantage of any belief that would encourage ordinary people to think that you were capable of superhuman strength, supernatural powers—indeed, that you were invincible?

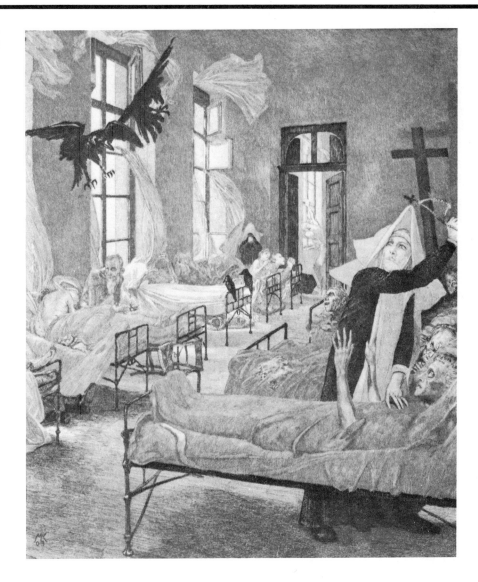

Nineteenth-century illustration depicting vampire bats attacking a hospital that is caring for victims of the plague.

From the 1971 Hammer film, Vampire Circus. *Anthony Corlan as the vampire,* *Emil, recoils in terror when confronted by a sharp knife in the shape of a crucifix.*

Chapter 2

CULTURAL DIFFERENCES AMONG VAMPIRES

For the most part nowadays, the general public's image of vampires is colored by Bram Stoker's 1897 novel *Dracula* and the numerous cinematic versions which have proliferated since the 1920s. To the nonexpert this is misleading. Even though, as you have seen in Chapter 1, there exists in Western civilization a substantial variety of vampires, the fact remains that these constitute only a single branch of the vampire family tree, as it were. It might be safe to say that all Western vampires are cousins. But what about those that exist in other cultures? Indeed, the lore of other peoples is replete with a hideous array of bloodsucking entities, some humanoid, some demonic, and most infinitely horrible.

But before examine the rest of the world, picture if you will some of the lesser-known European vampires. In Germany there is the Alp; best described as a nightmare demon, the Alp not only sucks the blood of its victims, but the nipples of men and women alike. The nightmare demon known to the Scandinavians as the Mara is one of several similar vampires in different parts of Europe. Generally she is a beautiful woman, not unlike a succubus. The southern Slavs assert that when a Mara (or Mora, as they call her) tastes the blood of a man, she becomes enamored of him and is unable to leave him. As a result she returns to him nightly to torment his sleep and send him nightmares.

There is a Bulgarian vampire with only one nostril and a long, sharp, pointed tongue. The German Neuntoter is a disgustingly ugly creature whose body exhales an excrementious stench. It is covered with hideous sores and is responsible for spreading the plague. A particularly dangerous variety of Romanian vampire is known as the Murony. Able to assume the form of almost any animal or bloodsucking insect, it preys upon unsuspecting victims who assume it to be nothing more than a natural creature. In its grave the Murony is instantly recognizable by its fangs, its sharp talons, and by the fact that fresh blood drips from its mouth, its eyes, its nose and ears. In Portugal the nightmare demon shares characteristics with both the werewolf and the vampire. According to a nineteenth-century scholar, Richard Andrée, ''At night she leaves her resting place and flies from home in the form of some gigantic night bird. The Bruxsas tryst with their diabolical lovers to seduce, terrify, and torment lonely travelers. On returning from their noctural journey of pleasure they suck the blood of their own children.'' The ancient Irish were quite direct about their native vampires, calling them ''Red Blood Suckers.'' When their graves were discovered, boulders and piles of heavy stones were placed over them to prevent the monsters from emerging at night to prey upon unsuspecting victims.

The Russian vampire is symbolically like its mother country, for it possesses qualities that span East and West. Like the vampire of the West, the Russian is an animated corpse that preys upon unwary victims. Unlike the Western vampire, however, the Russian variety is often a savagely homicidal corpse that lurks in graveyards and lures innocent passersby to their deaths. Not content with merely drinking their blood, Russian vampires rip their prey to shreds and devour them in the manner of the Arabian *ghul* or ghoul. So terrible is this vampire that when modern Russians use the term as a political pejorative the implication is far more grave then it appears on the surface.

One of the most fascinating pieces of vampire lore comes from Siberia. It deals with a folk hero name Itje, whose parents had been devoured by a fearful demon named Tunegusse. Itje escaped the monster by fleeing to the home of relations who lived in a distant desert. However, when he grew to manhood he returned to the place of his birth with the sworn intention of liberating his people from the clutches of the demon. Again and again he succeeded in killing this fierce eater of humans. But as often as he slew the fiendish creature, it was reborn to continue its depredations against its hapless victims. Seeing that his efforts were not successful, Itje decided to seek more effective means of

ridding the world of this scourge. He built a great roaring fire, fully intending to reduce his enemy to ashes. Upon felling it this time he consigned its corpse to the flames, but it was not consumed, even though it turned to ashes which began to cool. The demon's charred jaws snapped open and shut with ear-splitting grinding sounds that sent painful chills down the spines of all within hearing. Suddenly a disembodied voice like that of a roaring tornado shrieked out in piercing tones that even though the flames might consume its body, it would contrive to plague mankind forever afterward. Then, barely had the words died out when a mighty gust of wind swept up the ashes and scattered them across the skies. And as they spread out on the wings of the wind, they turned into swarms of mosquitoes, which flew in black clouds to the four corners of the earth, where they continue to suck the blood of mankind to this very day.

In order to fully comprehend the utter horror of the Chinese vampires, one must first gain some insight into the Chinese concept of the soul. According to Chinese belief, man is endowed with two souls. First, there is the superior soul, or the Hun. This is associated with the Shen, or good spirits. When it appears after death it is seen in the likeness of its possessor in life. The second soul, which is regarded as the inferior, is known as the P'o. It is thoroughly malignant and is associated with the nature of the Kuei, or evil spirits. It is believed to remain in the body of the deceased where, upon occasion, it is strong enough to prevent bodily decomposition and give the corpse the appearance of life. To quote from my book, *Passport to the Supernatural,* "The most dreaded of Chinese spirits are the vampires, or Ch'iang Shih. In behavior they resemble their Western counterparts, but they are more complicated, being demons associated with the P'o. They not only animate corpses and keep them

Vampir, *an 1895 lithograph by the Norwegian artist, Edvard Munch.*

from decaying, but can assemble an entire form from as little as an old skull or a few half-rotten bones. Their tenancy of corpses, of course, ensures the freshness of reanimated bodies for as long as they are able to remain. With blazing red eyes, they have razor-sharp talons, pale white or greenish hair all over the body, resembling mold or decay, and in addition to sucking blood from their victims, like ghouls they devour the flesh of the dead.''

In Japan, as in China, there is a veritable pantheon of evil spirits and demons. One of the most insidious is a monstrous vampire cat which sinks its fangs into the throat of its victim and sucks out the blood, then buries the body and transforms itself into the likeness of the dead person in order to prey upon his or her loved ones.

There is an ancient Japanese tale of such a cat. It plagued the household of a Nabeshima prince, one of the feudal lords of Hizen. First, it killed and assumed the shape of the prince's favorite concubine, a ravishing beauty named Otoyo. Next, it began visiting the prince nightly after casting a mysterious deep and dreamless sleep upon his royal guards. Then, during the darkest hours of the night it began sucking out the prince's blood. With the passage of time he grew weaker, became thin, and was overcome with lassitude. It was quickly apparent to all that he was the victim of some terrible debilitating sickness of mysterious origin.

A soldier in the Nabeshima army named Ito Soda, unwilling to stand by and see his master waste away, volunteered to stand guard by the prince's bedside at night so that he might determine if any sorcery was at work. When the vampire came that night Ito Soda, too, began to feel the all but irresistible drowsiness induced by the demon.

To prevent himself from succumbing, he drew a sharp dagger and plunged it into his own thigh, after which he twisted the hilt as hard as he could. The pain was so severe that the drowsiness left him at once.

Not long after that he became aware of a muffled figure creeping into his lord's chamber. Peering through the darkness, he soon distinguished the features of the most beautiful woman he had ever seen. At the sight of Ito Soda sitting there she started with alarm and demanded to know his identity and his reason for being present. He answered her questions and watched the disguised vampire with suspicion. Frustrated by his presence she finally withdrew from the chamber. Night after night she returned, but upon each occasion Ito Soda remained faithfully on guard, and before long the prince began to regain his strength.

Having been thwarted so often, the false concubine ceased her nightly visits. It soon occurred to Ito Soda that the other guards were no longer falling into their deep sleep every night at precisely the same hour. Furthermore, he no longer felt the familiar drowsiness himself. The realization struck him that the beautiful woman had indeed been a vampire. He revealed his suspicions to the prime minister and declared that it was his intention to confront the vampire in her chamber and kill her forthwith. That night, after dark, he gained entrance to her quarters on the pretence of bringing her a message. But instead of a letter he drew a long, sharp dagger and sprang at her. Retaining her guise of a beautiful maiden she seized a battle axe and swung it at Ito Soda in a deadly arc. But each time she lunged, he parried her thrusts, until she finally realized that she was unable

to surpass him in the warrior's art. At that moment, with a fearful shriek, she changed into a giant, shaggy cat, and without another sound, leaped through the window, vanishing into the night.

The prime minister and eight armed men who had been standing guard outside were taken by surprise. Despite the arrows they shot at the monster, it fled to the neighboring mountains, where it wreaked havoc among the dwellers there. Eventually, the prince assembled a great band of armed men, whereupon they tracked the demon down and killed it once and for all.

A romanticized French concept of the female vampire.

To describe the pantheon of demons that exist throughout the Orient would require an encyclopedia. Notable are the vampires of Malaysia. There we encounter vampires of quite an exotic nature. One of them, called the Langsuir, according to *The Vampire Papers,* "appears as a beautiful woman wearing a flowing green robe. Her nails are long, tapering, and sharp, and she has jet black hair that flows down to her ankles. In the back of her neck there is a hole through which she sucks the blood of children. She is believed to have once been a beautiful woman who, when her child was stillborn, was so overcome with grief that she flew away into the jungle and became a demon. In addition to the blood of children, she has an inordinate fondness for fish, and she often lurks near rivers so that she may steal from unsuspecting fishermen. She can be rendered harmless if she is captured, provided her captors follow the proper procedure. First her nails and hair must be cut short and the hair stuffed into the hole in her neck. Then she will become quite tame and behave as an ordinary woman. Women are in danger of becoming Langsuirs after death if they die in childbirth or immediately afterward. To prevent this, the mouth of the dead woman is filled with glass beads, eggs are placed in her armpits, and needles in the palms of her hands. By taking these precautions she cannot flap her arms to fly, open her mouth to shriek, and she will rest in her grave peacefully.''

Just as certain European vampires are believed to have the ability to metamorphose into bats and other creatures, so is the Langsuir believed to be able to change into an owl.

Another Malaysian vampire, the Pennanggalan, is far from beautiful. To quote once more from *The Vampire Papers,* ''she is one of the most repulsive vampires in the world and like so many others she favors young children as victims. According to legend she was once an old woman. One day while in the act of performing a religious duty, sitting at the time on the edge of a large vat of vinegar, she was suddenly startled by the appearance of a strange man. She jumped up so suddenly that she kicked herself under the chin with great violence and in the process separated her head from her body. With that, the head and its dangling entrails flew away to a treetop and lived forever afterward as a malicious demon. Another account of the Pennanggalan's origin tells us that she was once a woman who devoted herself to the study of witchcraft and black magic. She had a devil for a private tutor who taught her everything she wished to learn. Finally when her studies were completed she was able to separate her head from her body at will and fly about seeking victims whose blood she could suck. It is also believed that after she has satiated herself with the blood of her victims, the Pennanggalan's intestines are bloated and distended. Therefore when she returns to her house, in order to return to her body, she must soak her entrails in a large jar of vinegar so that they will shrink and fit properly. Since she favors children, especially newborn infants, elaborate precautions are taken by superstitious Malaysians when babies are born. Thorns are strung up around the windows and doors so that if she enters the house, she will catch her intestines on them and become hopelessly entangled. It is very important for those who believe to protect themselves from this she-vampire, for it is feared that if any blood or other liquid drips from her onto a living person the result will be dreadful sores and severe illness.'' It should be added that the custom of hanging thorns in doors and windows of houses is not peculiar to Malaysia. Precautions of a similar nature were commonplace among the ancient Greeks and among the Hungarians, the Serbs, and the Bohemians during the seventeenth and eighteenth centuries. These protections include buckthorn, whitethorn, briars, herbs, garlic, horseshoes, and crosses.

Still a third Malaysian vampire is quite unlike anything that exists elsewhere. It is the Polong, a tiny humanoid creature no more than an inch in length. The Polong always acts in conjunction with its familiar, the Pelesit, or cricket demon. The Pelesit has a razor-sharp tail with which it burrows into the victim's body. When the opening is large enough for the Polong to enter, the Pelesit signals by chirping. Once the Polong has gone into the body of its prey, the result is a dreadful insanity, during which the victim raves deliriously about cats. Unlike so many other vampires the Polong is not a former human or even a demon. It is created by deliberate sorcery. Traditionally one manufactures a Polong by collecting the blood of a murdered man in a bottle. The next step is to utter incantations and cast spells constantly for a week or more, during which time the Polong grows out of the blood. When it is ready to emerge it chirps like the Pelesit. It is then necessary to make a slight incision on the finger and stick it into the bottle every day in order that the creature will be properly nourished. The main function of the Polong is to go forth on orders from its master to kill enemies or drive them mad.

The Pelesit is made from the tongue of a dead infant. The child must be the first-born of a first-born mother, and it must be dead for less than forty days. According to tradition the body must be placed above an anthill in a clearing until it cries and sticks out its tongue. After the tongue is bitten off it must be placed in a coconut shell filled with water and cooked over a fire which has been built at a triple crossroad. After it has been properly steeped it must be buried on the spot. If all the procedures have been followed to the letter, the tongue will become a Pelesit.

One last Malaysian vampirelike demon is also created by means of sorcery. Named the Bajang, it usually assumes the shape of a weasel-like creature or a large lizard. It is usually made from the soul of an infant that has died at birth and has been freshly buried. This is customarily done by a malevolent sorcerer who comes to the grave in the dead of night, chants incantations, and induces the body to emerge. Like Polongs and Pelesits, Bajangs are used by their creators to attack enemies, who are then seized by fits of fainting and convulsions. A Bajang may be destroyed if one discovers its creator and kills him.

No discussion of Asian vampires is complete without mention of the Indian variety. Certainly the archetype of all Indian vampires is not a true vampire but a goddess, Kali, also known as Durga and Parvati, the latter names referring to her two benign aspects. She is the goddess of destruction, plagues, bloodthirstiness, death, and violence. Her idol is depicted as black and smeared with blood. She has immense fangs and bloodstained hands, yet paradoxically she has also been described as "terrible and beautiful, terribly beautiful." *The Vampire Papers* says: "She is depicted in Indian mythology as a dark woman with long flowing hair and four arms. In statues and drawings she holds a sword in one arm, and a severed head in the second; with the other two she beckons to her worshippers. Her adornments are as hideous as her nature. She wears dangling corpses for earrings and a necklace of human skulls. Kali's face is horrible to contemplate. Her eyes are blood red and her tongue hangs drunkenly out of her mouth.

"The head that Kali brandishes belongs to Raktavika, chief of the army of demons. In a furious battle between gods and demons, according to myth, Kali attacked this archdemon and smote him with every weapon at her disposal. Each drop of his blood generated a thousand giant demons as powerful as Raktavika himself. Kali ultimately defeated her enemy by drinking all of his blood. Then, glutted and sated by victory she embarked on a wild dance of joy that caused the entire earth to tremble.

This 19th-century engraving of a vampire's kiss depicts a bat-winged vampire, an image reflecting kinship with the South American vampire bat.

"Until they were stamped out by the British in the 1830s, the worshippers of Kali constituted a deadly menace in India. They were known as the Thugs, the word coming from the Hindi word meaning deceivers. They were greatly feared for they garrotted and strangled their victims before they robbed them of their possessions. Their murderous practices were called Thuggee and were developed to a fine art. Often individual members of the cult lived double lives. By day they were respectable, ordinary people. But after dark they became night stalkers and stranglers who left nothing but terror and death in their wake. In the early 1800s before they were wiped out as an organized confraternity it was estimated that they accounted for as many as 30,000 ritual murders per year. The heritage they left behind was a lasting one, for even today the term thug is commonly applied to murderers, thieves, and other criminals."

And according to knowledgeable Indians the cult of Kali has not died out entirely, for there are remote areas in India where Thuggee is still practiced.

One of the most terrifying vampire-demons of India is the Rakshasa. Described as extremely ugly, deformed, and colored either a bright blue, green, or yellow, it is dreadful to behold. Especially hideous are its eyes, long, gleaming slits. It animates dead bodies, eats human flesh, and perpetrates extensive acts of mischief, ranging from interference with religious rites to the theft of horses, for which it has an inordinate appetite. This latter trait was particularly serious in the days when horses were a principal means of transportation. Rakshasas have long sharp talons which are lethal, for anyone scratched by them is doomed to a painful death. Despite their loathsome fearfulness they are said to be fabulously rich, and they have been known on occasion to take a liking to certain humans, whom they make indescribably rich.

The Vetala is another Indian vampire-demon that lurks in the vicinity of tombs, lonely forests, and other places with a dark and sinister reputation. Like the Rakshasa, the Vetala animates corpses, but unlike it the Vetala does not change appearance. Vetalas have voracious appetites for human flesh, and tear their prey to pieces with supernatural strength. They are sometimes seen hanging upside down from the limbs of trees like bats. They, too, sometimes display benign feelings for humans and help them in times of distress. An example of this can be found in one of the great Indian epic sagas, translated by Sir Richard Burton as *Vikram and the Vampire*. The hero, King Trivikramasena, is a semimythical character who occupies a place in Indian tradition roughly parallel to that of King Arthur in our own.

In the story the king falls into the clutches of an evil yogi, a follower of Kali, whose plans include using the king as an innocent tool in

GREEK WORD FOR VAMPIRE, VRYKOLAKAS, AND ITS DEFINITION

No plague more terrible or more harmful to man can well be thought of or conceived. The name has been given him from a vile filth. Boύpκα *means black mud, not any kind of mud, but feculent mud that is slimy and oozing with excrementious sewerage so that it exhales a most noisome stench.* Aάkkos *is a ditch or cloaca in which foulness of this kind collects and reeks amain.*

Leo Allatius (1586-1669), Greek scholar and theologian, who served as Vatican librarian until his death. From the treatise *De Quorundum Graecorum Opinionatibus,* 1645.

his sorcery, which will eventually result in the yogi's becoming ruler of the world. An integral part of the story concerns Trivikramasena's involvement with a Vetala, which he must take down from a tree and carry from place to place every night for a prescribed period of time. Each night the Vetala presents the king with a riddle. If he is able to answer it, the vampire permits him to live. If he fails, however, his fate is to be torn to pieces and devoured. Naturally, he answers all the riddles successfully, outfoxes the malevolent yogi, and resumes his rightful place in the order of things.

Nowhere in the present-day world does the supernatural play a more important role in everyday life than in Africa. It is not surprising, then, that blood should be an integral part of African cultures. The Masai, for instance, include blood as a major part of their diet, although it is the blood of cattle, not human beings. According to Lynn Myring's *Vampires, Werewolves, and Demons*, "Many African tribes also made offerings of blood to the ghosts and spirits of their ancestors. Some spirits seemed to be happy with animal blood, but if they were not honored by blood sacrifice they would return and spread illness and death among living relatives. Ghosts became more unpleasant and dangerous the longer they were dead and it was important not to offend them. Sometimes the spirit returned as a ferocious man-eating animal. . . . Ghosts were sometimes said to cause death by eating the victim's heart and liver."

GREEK CURSES BELIEVED TO DOOM THE RECIPIENTS TO BECOME VAMPIRES AFTER DEATH

1. May the earth not receive him!
2. May the ground not consume him!
3. May the earth not digest thee!
4. May the black earth spew thee up!
5. Mayest thou remain incorrupt!
6. May the earth not loose thee! [i.e., may the body not decompose.]
7. May the ground reject thee!
8. Mayest thou become in the grave like rigid wood!
9. May the ground reject him wholly!

According to Freudian disciple Ernest Jones, these curses may be undone by the *person who may have inadvertently uttered them in moments of anger. This is customarily attended to on the deathbed of the individual who invoked them. "A vessel of water is brought to the bedside and he throws into it a handful of salt, and when this is dissolved the sick man sprinkles with the lymph all those who are present saying, 'As this salt dissolves so may my curses dissolve.' This ceremony absolves all persons whom he may have cursed in his lifetime from the evil of a ban which after death he would no longer be able to revoke."*

*Silhouette of Count Orlock, from the
1921 version of* Nosferatu.

Chapter 3

THE REAL-LIFE DRACULA

The stories of his ferocious savageries exceed
belief.

Encyclopedia Britannica (11th Ed.)

It is hard to imagine that there is anyone who has not heard of Dracula. But it was not until 1972, with the publication of the book *In Search of Dracula* by Raymond T. McNally and Radu Florescu, that the story of the historical Dracula became fairly well known beyond the relatively limited circle of specialists in East European history. Even now, the average person thinks Dracula was a bloodsucking Transylvanian vampire count who looked and sounded like Bela Lugosi or Christopher Lee, depending on the age of the person you ask.

Actually the true story bears no resemblance to Bram Stoker's novel, even though the principal character is based loosely on someone who actually lived. Although the Romanian government has been striving to rehabilitate the reputation of Dracula and make him into a great national hero, the fact remains that he was actually a monster incarnate whose niche in history is alongside such kindred spirits as Caligula, Nero, Jack the Ripper, and Hitler. In a sense his story begins exactly eighty-four years before the discovery of America.

In 1408, King Sigismund of Hungary, who later became Holy Roman emperor, established a knightly order—the Order of the Dragon. Its members wore an official uniform which consisted of a short green cloak and a bright scarlet tunic. The insignia of the order was a double gold chain with a coiled dragon. It was required of all knights in the order to wear the dragon whenever they appeared in public. Any violation of this rule resulted in a fine, the sum being equivalent to the cost of five masses.

In time the order became, in a sense, a very exclusive political club, claiming among its members men belonging to the noblest houses of Europe. As the order grew, so did its political power. It is recorded that on one occasion, when Sigismund journeyed to Paris, he rode at the head of a procession consisting of eight hundred knights of the order, resplendent in their full regalia.

In 1431 Dracula's father, Vlad Dracul (the devil), was invested with the Order of the Dragon by Sigismund, now Holy Roman emperor, in Nuremburg, the site of his court.

At the same time he was made voivode or prince of Wallachia, a district which borders on Transylvania, in the eastern part of present-day Romania. The title voivode referred to a warrior prince rather than one who inherited his title. Since the principal purpose of the Order of the Dragon was to fight the Turks, Dracul's investiture bound him to joining the fight as well as to holding and defending Wallachia. He was not able to formally ascend his throne until the year 1436, when he succeeded in seizing it from the reigning prince by force. After strengthening his grip on Wallachia, Dracul, a shrewd politician, saw that the Turkish sultan, Murad II, was becoming more powerful than his adversary, the Holy Roman emperor. Renouncing his oath in 1438, he allied himself with the Turks and joined them in a number of bloody invasions of Transylvania to plunder, murder, rape, and burn. Yet, as a Christian, he did what he could to save the lives of his coreligionists.

As a result of this the sultan became suspicious of Dracul, summoned him to Constantinople with his two sons, and accused him of disloyalty. To avoid execution and to retain his throne, Dracul pledged further loyalty to the sultan and left his two sons as hostages. It was at this time that the older son, Dracula, received the education that contributed so much to his becoming the bloody tyrant he eventually became.

McNally and Florescu write:

"Dracula from that time onward held human nature in low esteem. Life was cheap—after all, his own was constantly threatened—and morality was nonessential in matters of state. He needed no Machiavelli to instruct him in the amorality of politics.

"He also developed during those years, as related by his Turkish captors,

a reputation for treachery, cunning, insubordination, and brutality, and inspired fright in his own guards, in contrast to his brother's sheepish subserviency. Two other traits were entrenched in Dracula's psyche because of the plot into which father and sons had been ensnared. One was suspicion; never again would he trust himself to the Turks or for that matter to any man, whether friend or foe. The other was revengefulness; Dracula would not forget, nor forgive, those whether high or low who crossed him; indeed this became a family trait."

In December of the year 1447, Dracul the father was assassinated. His death was a direct result of his own treachery, for after returning to the throne he switched sides again: he broke his vow to the Turkish sultan and again swore loyalty to the Holy Roman emperor. It is a miracle that his son Dracula was not executed for his father's final betrayal of the Turks.

Staging a daring escape from Turkey in 1448 Vlad Dracula made his way to Wallachia and assumed the throne briefly, for a period of two months. He was only about twenty years old at the time and fearing that his father's assassins might make an attempt on his life, fled to Moldavia, a northern province of Romania which was ruled by his uncle Prince Bogdan. When Bogdan was assassinated in 1451, Dracula returned to Transylvania and boldly offered to throw in his lot with Janos Hunyadi, the celebrated Hungarian statesman-warrior, and also the man who had been responsible for his father's assassination. Though neither trusted the other, it proved to be an association of mutual convenience. Dracula remained Hunyadi's disciple until 1456. After Hunyadi's death during an outbreak of the plague, Dracula was formally invested with the voivodeship of Wallachia. There he embarked on a stormy reign which was to last until the year 1462, when he was deposed by the Turks. He fled to Hungary and sought asylum with Hunyadi's son, King Mathias. To his surprise and consternation, Mathias had him taken in chains to Budapest, where he remained a political prisoner for the next twelve years.

There is no precise explanation as to why Mathias imprisoned Dracula, but it is safe to assume that it was in response to pressure from the German population of the Transylvanian city of Sibiu, where the Wallachian prince had once lived between his reigns. The city was regarded as a safe haven from the Turks, who were constantly waging war against their western neighbors. And what was the complaint of Sibiu's inhabitants against their fellow Transylvanian? Some years earlier, in a vicious act of deliberate savagery, Dracula, at the head of twenty thousand Wallachian troops, swooped down upon the unsuspecting city to pillage, loot, torture, and slay some ten thousand of its residents. It was said afterward that the ferocity of Dracula's incursion made earlier assaults by the Turks pale by comparison.

Incredible as it may seem, Dracula married King Mathias's sister during his captivity. In November of 1476 he was permitted to return to the throne of Wallachia, but his bloody career was finally ended one month later, when he was killed in a battle with the Turks outside of Budapest. He was forty-five years old. As with so many other aspects of Dracula's life, there is more than one version of how he actually died. According to one account, the tide of battle had begun to turn in his favor. Disguising himself as a Turk, he climbed a hill to get a better view of the Turkish forces being bested by his troops. Suddenly, so the story goes, he was spotted by several of his own men, who mistook him for an authentic Turk. Though he fought bravely, managing to kill five of his attackers in the process, he was finally slain by his own men. Another version states that he was killed by a group of personal enemies and boyars. Whoever actually ended Dracula's life, it is known that he was decapitated—possibly after his death—and his head was dispatched to Constantinople, where it was placed on public display by the Turks to advertise the fact that their old enemy was dead.

From the foregoing sketchy outline of Vlad Dracula's life, it would be easy enough to assume that he was just another minor ruler of a small principality. But from accounts of the atrocities he perpetrated, we know today what a bloodthirsty, tyrannical fiend he was in reality. The names by which he has come to be known provide us with the initial clues to his true nature. Dracul, the name applied to his father, had the double meanings of devil and dragon. It is not inconceivable that the superstitious peasants of his father's time, seeing the dragon emblem, automatically associated him with the devil. However, we know that Vlad Dracul, too, was an extremely harsh man, so it is quite likely that the term was used with the double meaning firmly in mind. The name Dracula, that is, Dracul with the letter a added, translates as "the son of Dracul," nothing more. And it was primarily by this name that he was known during his lifetime. There was still another name which he acquired, as specific as Dracula: it was Tepes, meaning "the impaler." How did he earn this ominous nickname? The answer is chillingly simple. Dracula's favorite means of punishing those who displeased him was to impale them alive on a stake. He preferred to use stakes with slightly blunted points, so that the victims would die slowly and thereby endure a maximum amount of suffering.

This well-known rendition of Vlad Tepes, or Vlad the Impaler, Voivode of Wallachia, does not do the man justice. Although he is generally regarded by historians as a cynical hypocrite as well as a tyrannical monster, he was, according to all contemporary accounts, a relatively handsome man.

McNally and Florescu discuss Dracula's characteristic method of torturing his victims: "There were various forms of impalement depending upon age, rank, or sex. . . . There were also various geometric patterns in which the impaled were displayed. Usually the victims were arranged in concentric circles and in the outskirts of cities where they could be viewed by all. There were high spears and low spears according to rank. There was impalement from above—feet upwards; and impalement from below—head upwards; or through the heart or navel. There were nails in people's heads, maiming of limbs, blinding, strangulation, burning, the cutting of noses and ears, and of sexual organs in the case of women, scalping and skinning, exposure to the elements or to wild animals, and boiling alive."

The motivation behind Dracula's impalement of victims was often so trivial as to defy belief. Frequently individuals were impaled on the whim of an instant. It is said that once he had a woman impaled for making her husband's shirt too short. During the time that he was committing his atrocities in Transylvania, sometime between 1459 and 1461, he is known to have impaled as many as twenty thousand prisoners, including Bulgarians, Germans, Hungarians, Romanians, and Turks. This forest of impaled corpses was located near the citadel of Giurgiu on the Danube River. When Mohammed II of Turkey and his troops encountered the grisly spectacle, they were sickened and demoralized.

Not long after Dracula assumed the throne of Wallachia in 1456, having assembled some five hundred boyars along with a number of prominent churchmen, he asked the assembled nobles how many Wallachian reigns they had known in their lifetime. They were an arrogant group, for often, in the past, it was they who dictated to the voivode, not the reverse. Dracula knew this and was determined to show them once and for all who ruled. He also knew that among them—though he did not know their precise identities—were the men responsible for his father's assassination. After each of the boyars had answered Dracula's question, most displaying a rather light attitude toward the throne, he ordered them surrounded, seized, and dragged outside, where five hundred of them were impaled and their corpses left to rot and be slowly picked to pieces by crows. It was an object lesson long remembered by the boyars who had been fortunate enough not to be present.

One of Dracula's best-known depravities occurred on April 2, 1459, in the city of Brasov. Before the sun set that spring day, thousands of the Saxon townsfolk were impaled in a circle around Dracula and an assemblage of his boyars as they feasted in a clearing near a church. An old German woodcut shows Dracula sitting at a table, surrounded by bodies on pales, as henchmen before him dismember the bodies of victims. The text of the pamphlet upon which the woodcut appears reads, ''Here begins a very cruel frightening story about a wild bloodthirsty man, Dracula voivode. How he impaled people and roasted them and with their heads boiled in a kettle, and how he skinned people and hacked them to pieces like a head of cabbage. He also roasted children of mothers and they had to eat their children themselves.

And many other horrible things are written in this tract and also in which land he ruled.''

How accurate all the specific accusations are is difficult to ascertain. There is ample evidence, however, to support assertions that most allegations against him were based on documented fact.

As the self-appointed guardian of public morals, Dracula committed some of the most atrocious slaughters in the name of morality. Unfaithful wives, unchaste widows, and unmarried women who lost their virginity were subjected to punishments of such vicious depravity that it is difficult to picture them as having been conceived and carried out by a supposedly civilized man. Women were skinned alive, body and skin being displayed in public on separate pales. Sexual organs were mutilated and upon occasion nipples were sliced off. Sometimes a long red hot stake of iron was thrust into the vagina, up through the body, and out of the victim's mouth.

Subject to bursts of whimsy, Dracula was known to set up situations in which people were in danger of falling into fatal traps sprung by their own tongues. Those with wit and discretion, adept in the art of cautious flattery, survived. Those not so fortunate would end up on a stake. An anecdote tells of how one of Dracula's boyars, unable to bear the stench emanating from a particularly bloody slaughter, held his nose. Seeing this Dracula immediately ordered the man to be impaled himself, but on a pole which was higher than the rest so that, as the boyar died, he would not be bothered by the stench of death around him. Insistent on total obediance and absolute acceptance of all his "accomplishments," he once impaled a monk who openly disapproved of the voivode's methods upon seeing several rows of impaled corpses in the castle courtyard. On another occasion two Turkish envoys refused to doff their turbans in accordance with Romanian custom. To remove them, they explained, was contrary to their own customs. Dracula, being a man who firmly believed that when in Romania, one did as the Romanians did, in a cold-blooded act of one-upmanship ordered the turbans nailed to the envoys' heads. By so doing, he explained sarcastically, he indicated how broadminded he was by personally reinforcing this foreign custom in his own court.

Such anecdotes about the count and his deeds abound, not only in Romanian lore but in that of the Russians, the Germans, and the Turks. Many of them are sufficiently similar to each other as to indicate their essential truth, whereas some accounts appear to be purely apocryphal. With the exception of some Romanian tales, which tend to paint him as a cruel but caring folk hero, most, regardless of their origin, agree in describing his atrocities in a veritable catalogue of horrors. But that is understandable. Those who had the strongest reasons to hate him were bound to give him a bad press.

One of the stories about him, which reinforces the assertion that a dominant portion of the inner man was a sadistic killer, appeared in a report by the Russian ambassador to the court of King Mathias. It was based on the ambassador's observations during the time that Dracula was a prisoner in Budapest. He apparently made friends with his guards and arranged for them to bring him a steady supply of small animals, including frogs, mice,

rats, and birds. Sometimes he tortured them by impalement on miniature stakes which he then arranged in rows, just as he did on a larger scale with human victims. At other times, for variety, he would content himself with cutting the unfortunate creatures to pieces. One of his favorite pastimes, according to the Russian, was to pluck chickens and savor their pain as they ran in circles screeching with terror. When he tired of this he would slit their throats and watch them bleed to death as they hopped about.

A sanctimonious man as well as a tyrant with no regard for the value of human life, he once said, "I am the holiest man ever born of woman." His rationale was simple: had he not made many martyrs and saints, having been instrumental in sending hordes of souls to heaven? Physically, the Impaler was an imposing-looking man. He has been described as stocky and powerfully built. His large green eyes had an intense, almost mad expression emphasized by bushy black eyebrows. Long, curly black hair hung down around his bull's neck, and he had a ruddy complexion. His nose was long and thin, with distended nostrils, and his lips were topped by a droopy black moustache.

Although there is no historical evidence that Vlad Dracula ever personally drank blood or was in any way a vampire, we know for a fact that when Bram Stoker wrote his classic novel, *Dracula*, he used Vlad as a role-model. In the text, Dr. Van Helsing specifically says, "He must, indeed, have been that Voivode Dracula who won his name against the Turk, over the great river on the very frontier of Turkey-land. If it be so, then was he no common man; for in that time, and for centuries after, he was spoken of as the cleverest and the most cunning, as well as the bravest of the sons of the 'land beyond the forest.' That mighty brain and that iron resolution went with him to his

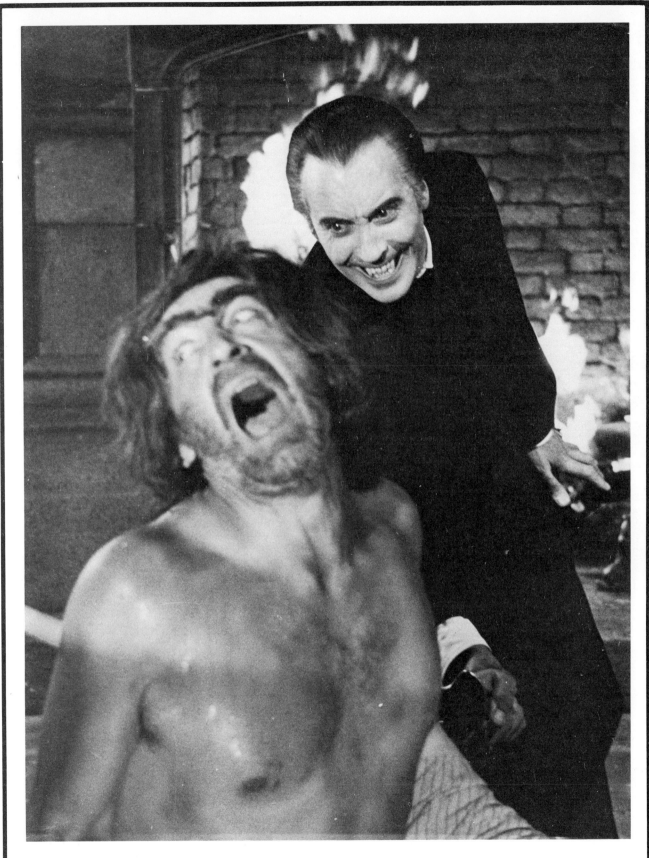

In the 1970 Hammer film, Scars of Dracula, *Christopher Lee, as the inde-* *structible count, prepares to savage one* *of his hapless victims.*

grave, and are even now arrayed against us. The Draculas were, says Arminius, a great and noble race, though now and again were scions who were held by their coevals [contemporaries] to have had dealings with the Evil One. They learned his secrets in the Schoolmance, amongst the mountains over Lake Hermanstadt, where the devil claims the tenth scholar as his due. In the records are such words as 'stregoica'—witch, 'ordog' and 'pokol'—Satan and Hell; and in one manuscript this very Dracula is spoken of as 'wampyr.'"

Obviously, Stoker wanted to choose a prototype for his vampire count who was synonymous with horror and blood. Perhaps he was unable to find a real vampire, but clearly his choice of Vlad the Impaler was a good one.

Artist's rendition of Dracula emerging from castle after nightfall.

A captive female vampire is threatened by one of the good guys in the 1974 Columbia-Warner release, The Satanic Rites of Dracula.

In the 1971 Hammer film, Countess Dracula, *Ingrid Pitt played the title role,* *based loosely on the real-life "vampire countess," Elisabeth Bathory.*

Chapter 4
LIVING VAMPIRES PAST AND PRESENT

As we know, the true vampire is "undead," existing in a limbo that is neither life nor death. Throughout history, however, there have been living vampires, whose lust for blood has driven them to the heights of unspeakable depravity. Since to tell about all of them would require a book in itself, we shall limit the present narrative to some of the better-known examples, whose careers earned them a permament niche in the archives of vampires.

Elisabeth Bathory

Certainly the most notorious of living vampires was the Hungarian Countess Elisabeth Bathory, whose unsavory career spanned the late sixteenth and early seventeenth centuries. Born into one of the oldest noble house of Hungary, her family crest bore the old draconian symbol adopted by Holy Roman Emperor Sigismund for the Order of the Dragon. At various times in history the Bathorys were a force to be reckoned with; the family included cardinals, bishops, government ministers, judges, even kings. By the beginning of the sixteenth century, however, like so many other inbred noble Europeans, they had become decadent, and many of them were involved in an assorted array of scandals. There were sado-masochists, satanists, lesbians, homosexuals, orgiasts, poisoners, and heretics. To make matters worse the Bathory clan had a wide streak of madness in its genes. Indeed, the family tree bore a rich harvest of psychotics, eccentrics, and other misfits. None, however, was able to match the extremities reached by the Countess Elisabeth, who was born on one of the family's sprawling estates in the foothills of the Carpathian mountains in the year 1560. As a child, she was exposed to all of the grisly folklore concerning vampires, werewolves, ghosts, and demons. When in her teens she was initiated into the arcane rites of witchcraft by her uncle, a devout satanist. At about the same time she fell under the spell of her sado-masochistic aunt, Klara, who also happened to be one of the most notorious lesbians in all of Hungary.

Young Elisabeth blossomed early into a ravishing beauty. Possessing a voluptuous figure, she had waist-length raven tresses, slightly slanted luminous amber eyes, high cheekbones, full sensuous lips, and a smooth creamy complexion. She had the body of an angel and the soul of a devil.

Despite the lesbian orgies in which she indulged with her aunt, Countess Elisabeth was not averse to sexual dalliance in the more traditional vein. At the age of ten her father died and she was officially engaged to Count Ferencz Nadasdy, a dark, handsome man often referred to as the "Black Lord," who considered himself more of a fighter than a lover. In 1574 she became pregnant by a mysterious stranger, probably a local peasant boy, and gave birth to an illegitimate daughter, who was secretly and permanently shipped off—interestingly enough, to Wallachia, the old domain of Dracula.

After her marriage to Count Nadasdy, Elisabeth and her husband moved to a gloomy, isolated castle in Csejthe. It was one of sixteen fortresses they jointly owned and was located atop a barren mountain in the southwestern region of Hungary, today a part of Czechoslovakia. Even now, legends of a chilling nature are whispered by the peasants of that district concerning the bloody vampire countess.

A strong-willed young woman, she refused to assume her husband's name at the time of her marriage. This apparently did not bother him, as he was more concerned with keeping abreast of the latest war. Wars were much more exciting than life in Castle Csejthe, and far more profitable.

In her new home, Elisabeth had little to do but try on her numerous gowns, have servants dress her hair, and preen before the looking-glass, fondling her jewels. She also experimented with assorted unguents and creams to assure the preservation of her flawless skin. In the absence of Count Nadasdy she amused herself with elegantly fashioned sex toys imported from Italy, but finding these less than responsive, after a time she embarked on a series of torrid affairs, changing lovers the way other women change clothes.

Something of a hypochondriac, she began to experiment with drugs, potions, powders, and noxious herbal brews, all of which only tended to exacerbate her unstable mental condition. Under the influence of her Aunt Klara, she indulged in acts of sado-masochistic cruelty by torturing female servants. It is difficult to imagine the savage punishments she inflicted on her hapless attendants, such as burning their genitals with candle flames, and even sewing shut the mouths of girls who chattered too much.

It did no good for the servants to appeal to the master of the castle on the infrequent occasions when he was present. He was far more concerned with his own little harem of pretty peasant wenches than with the domestic horrors perpetrated by his wife. After all, who cared about peasants and servants? They could be replaced. His attitude suited the countess perfectly. She thrived on torture, and rumors began to circulate among the servants and beyond the castle walls that she was a witch and a vampire.

It dawned on the count one day that it was time to perpetuate the family name. In no uncertain terms he ordered his wife to provide him with an heir or two, adding jocularly that if she was as accomplished a witch as the

A succubus, or female spirit of the night, seducing a helpless sleeper.

peasants asserted, it should be a simple matter for her. Oddly enough she gave her husband no trouble in the matter and over the next years produced a daughter and three sons. Motherhood had no softening influence on Elisabeth Bathory and her tastes for refined torture grew stronger. Her three favorite servants were an ugly wetnurse named Ilona Joo, an even uglier hag named Dorrtya Szentes, or Dorko, and a retarded cripple named Janos Ujvary, better known as Ficzko. Enlisting their enthusiastic assistance, Elisabeth began exploring the possibilities of more original, more terrible means of torturing those who aroused her displeasure. She employed such implements as sharp knives, molten wax, and red hot irons. She was known, upon occasion, to thrust a glowing pleating iron down the throat of a girl who did not sew well enough to suit her. Again and again, Elisabeth's mother-in-law attempted to dissuade her from such vicious behavior, but the poor woman's pleas fell on deaf ears. Occasionally even the count himself registered an objection, reminding her that others of her rank had been hanged for such deeds.

On January 4, 1604, Count Nadasdy died. After the funeral solemnities were disposed of, Elisabeth felt a sense of excitement. She was now complete mistress of her domain. No longer was there anyone who could give her a single order. Her children were sent off to be educated and she was now able to devote all of her time to black magic, new lovers, and satanism. Before long she banished her mother-in-law and got rid of all but a select group of servants whose talents and inclinations especially suited her warped requirements. Ilona Joo, Dorko, and Ficzko were given the responsibility of recruiting victims. The loathsome trio would travel around to remote villages, where the name of their mistress had not become synonymous with evil and terror. For small sums of money or cheap gifts they would convince the poverty-stricken mothers of nubile young peasant girls to send their daughters off to a life of security in service to the mighty house of Bathory.

One day, while riding across the countryside with one of her handsome young lovers, Elisabeth noticed a wrinkled old woman alongside the road. Contemplating the woman's extreme ugliness, the countess burst into a nasty laugh and said to her lover, "How would you like it if I were to order you to embrace an old hag like that?" He promptly replied that to be forced into such an act would revolt him. Infuriated at the cruel jest at her expense, the old woman turned, and glaring at the beautiful countess, she said, "Mock me if you will, mistress of Csejthe, but one day you, too, will be as I am now!" The thought horrified Elisabeth. She had never contemplated the idea of growing old. She became obsessed with the horror of it. Her nightmares led her through halls of mirrors in which she saw herself as hideous, shriveled, and wrinkled—ugly beyond her waking imagination, her ugliness exaggerated by the beauty of her jewels, her satins, her silks and brocades. Now, though she was still one of the most celebrated beauties in Europe, she began devoting more time to the preservation of that beauty.

One day a personal maid, while combing the countess's hair, accidentally pulled too hard. In a violent outburst of temper, Elisabeth struck the girl across the face with such a powerful blow that it drew blood. Without thinking she tasted it and felt a strange exhilaration. Then, upon rubbing the remaining blood over her face, she came to the conclusion that it had made her more beautiful than ever before. That single act sealed the fate of hundreds of future victims.

Elisabeth knew that the girl she had struck was a virgin and it suddenly occurred to her that she had discovered the secret of eternal youth—that if she bathed in the blood of virgins there would be no end to her beauty and vitality. Summoning two of her strongest henchmen, she had the girl seized and stripped. As the unfortunate creature screamed for mercy she was dragged into the countess's bath chamber. Then, as she was held upside down by her heels over a tub, her throat was slashed like a sheep in a slaughterhouse. Eventually she stopped struggling when all her blood had dripped out. Elisabeth then dismissed the two men, with orders to get rid of the body. Then she undressed and bathed in the fresh, warm blood. She had discovered a pleasure that surpassed any she had ever known.

It now became necessary for her to have a steady supply of virgins in order to take her frequent, ritual bloodbaths. Thriving on this steady supply of blood, and convinced that it was solely responsible for her good looks and energy, the countess began making trips to the imperial court in Vienna. There she occupied a house that was particularly suited to her fiendish nature. Located on Schulerstrasse, a dark narrow street that later became known as *Blutgasse*, or Blood Alley, as a result of her periodic residence there, it was a sinister place with crypts and catacombs below the street level. In the perpetually dark depths of this ill-omened place the countess arranged for each victim to be placed in a cylindrical iron cage suspended

Sigismund, the Holy Roman emperor.

from the ceiling. As it was raised, a series of spiked hoops contracted mechanically, thereby slashing the victim inside to death. Clad in a virginal white gown, Elisabeth sat below on a stool, bathing in the shower of fresh blood which she drank and smeared all over her exposed parts until she was swept to the heights of orgasmic pleasure.

She soon grew bored with this relatively simple torture device and designed something even more diabolical. Known as "the iron virgin," it was built by a clockmaker in Germany and installed in a dungeon of Castle Csejthe. The "virgin" was a lifesize cast-iron replica of a pretty naked girl, painted in flesh tones, with long, flowing blonde hair, a smiling, movable mouth with human teeth, and a tuft of human pubic hair. Imbedded around the neck was a necklace of precious gems which in reality were buttons that activated the mechanism. A victim would be forced to hug the terrible device, when suddenly the arms would rise and seize the hapless girl in an iron embrace; then shutters located in the breasts would open and out would come five steel blades to impale the victim in such a way as to permit servants to collect the blood which drained from the body. It was gathered in basins and taken to the countess's bath chamber in time for her morning ablution of blood.

One day Elisabeth came to the conclusion that the blood baths were not as effective as she had originally believed them to be. She was seized by the fear of losing her beauty. It was then that she was convinced by one of her associates that what she really needed was the blood of young noble women, not common peasants. It was the beginning of a series of events which would lead to her eventual downfall.

In the year 1610 twenty-five daughters of minor nobles were brought to Castle Csejthe under the erroneous assumption that they were to be nothing more than genteel companions to one of the highest-ranking noblewomen in the land. In two weeks, all twenty-five of them were dead, victims of Countess Bathory's blood lust. For the first time in her career the haughty Elisabeth was guilty, under Hungarian law, of a crime punishable by death. The daughters of peasants had no rights, and therefore to torture and kill them might be regarded as a rather nasty and unladylike way to pass the time, but certainly not as a serious offense. But to perpetrate the same depravities on daughters of the nobility was a different story entirely.

In any case, where were more blue-blooded girls to come from? The wily Ilona Joo and her two cohorts now took to procuring peasant girls, bathing them, dressing them, making them up so that they looked like noblewomen, and then bringing them to the castle under cover of darkness. Meanwhile, since rumors of her dark deeds had spread to the court of the king himself, it was only a matter of time before Elisabeth's bloody career was terminated. A man named Megyery, who was one of the many enemies she had made over the years, had strong suspicions as to the true nature of her secret activities. He was respected by the king and began working feverishly to gather concrete evidence against Countess Bathory. In 1610 an event occurred which gave him the ammunition he needed. Elisabeth's henchmen made the error of kidnapping a girl from a nearby village whose parish priest gave strong credence to the many rumors he had heard about the lady of Csejthe. There had been too many disappearances, too many young women who had gone to the castle never to be heard from again. He made it a point to see that whatever information he had was delivered to the king himself. The king immediately ordered an investigation. It happened that the rumors included alleged

One of the beautiful female "undead's"
in Jean Rollin's 1969 film, La Vampire
Nue.

verbatim accounts of certain withering curses Elisabeth had uttered. One of these curses had specifically mentioned the monarch. That was all he had to hear. Summoning his prime minister, Count Gyorgy Thurzo, a member of the Bathory family and cousin of Countess Elisabeth, he roared, "Not only is your cousin a bloodthirsty murderous witch, she is guilty of high treason!"

Thus, on the night of December 10, 1610, a detachment of troops led by Count Thurzo attacked the castle and interrupted an orgy of unbelievable debauchery. The countess was confined to a tower room and all her retainers were dragged off to prison in chains.

The trial itself began in January 1611 and lasted until the end of February. Presiding over a panel of twenty judges was the chief justice of Hungary himself. Because of Countess Bathory's rank and high political connections the tribunal was conducted in secret. Thurzo later commented to members of the family, "I should have killed her on the spot had I obeyed my own instincts. But in the interests of the defendant's house of Nadasdy justice was carried out in secret. For if she had to be judged by a public tribunal then all of Hungary would know of these murders."

The king ordered that the trial be treated as a straight murder case, not one of witchcraft or vampirism. When the witnesses began giving their testimony, the judges were horrorstruck. Eventually the final tally of victims came in and the Countess Bathory was accused of personally murdering six hundred and fifty girls, many of whom she had bitten to death in the neck.

All of the accused were adjudged guilty as charged. All except the countess, Ilona Joo, and Dorko were beheaded. Ilona Joo had her fingers torn from her hands by red-hot pincers before being burned at the stake. Although the king was all for beheading the countess at once, he gave in to pressure from her family, who would gladly have killed her themselves, but who felt that to subject her to the executioner would bring disgrace upon them. A compromise was reached. The fifty-year-old Elisabeth, her fabled beauty now faded, was placed under heavy guard in her castle and walled up alive in a small tower room. Slits were left for air and the passage of food and water. Her permanent confinement accomplished, the Hungarian nobles returned to their own world of intrigues and purged the vampire countess from their minds.

Peasants in the surrounding area, however, were not quite certain that they had seen the last of her. Convinced that she was indeed a witch and a vampire, they were certain that she would pass through the stone walls as a wisp of smoke or tiny creature and continue to wreak vengeance on them. Fortunately nothing of the sort happened. After four years in solitary confinement she died unrepentant. Over the years she had kept meticulous notes in a diary, listing virtually every girl she had ever tortured and slain. In most instances the entries were followed by brief comments such as, "She was very beautiful, but too small," or "She died too quickly."

Superstitions, however, die hard. Though Csejthe Castle is nothing but a ruin today, it may still be seen by visitors to the present-day Czech town of Chactice. If arrangements can be made to visit the ruin, a single walled-up room may still be found amid the decay. In that crumbling sepulcher Elisabeth Bathory lies, a heap of moldering bones.

Fritz Haarmann—The Hanover Vampire

There is no doubt that if Fritz Haarmann had lived in the fifteenth or sixteenth centuries he would have been tortured to death and burned at the stake as a werewolf. The verdict would have been based purely on a technicality because Haarmann only acted like a werewolf. In reality he was a vampire.

He was not the sort of vampire, however, to have been portrayed on the screen by the late Bela Lugosi or by Christopher Lee. He did not emerge from a grave at night to prowl the dark in search of victims. He did not even look like the archetypal vampire. He was a fat homosexual with an unpleasant disposition and a high-pitched, squeaky voice.

Haarmann was born in 1879, the son of a locomotive stoker with an evil disposition and a submissive, defeated *hausfrau.* With good reason Haarmann grew up worshiping his mother and hating his badtempered, quarrelsome father. A shy child, he was frightened of boys his own age and preferred remaining home to help his mother with housework or sewing, to dress in girls' clothes, and to play with his sister's dolls. He was a poor student; nevertheless, he managed to get through military school, after which he joined the army and actually succeeded in receiving a satisfactory rating as a soldier from his superior officers. His military career did not last long, however, and after a severe case of sunstroke at age seventeen he returned to civilian life.

Although his father was able to get him a job after his military discharge, he was arrested for molesting small boys and committed to a mental hospital. It was a hell-hole, for afterward he stated publicly, "Cut off my head, don't send me back to the madhouse." Somehow he managed to escape six months

after his confinement and fled to Switzerland, where he remained for two years without getting into trouble.

He then returned to Hanover and went back to live with his family. Soon he began quarreling violently with his father, with whom it was impossible for him to get along. For a brief time he was engaged to be married but he soon broke the engagement and tried again to take up the military life, joining the crack tenth Jäger battalion of the German army. Apparently this regimented existence agreed with him. He was regarded as an ideal soldier, his officers were satisfied with his conduct, and had he not become ill and received a medical discharge, society might have been better off.

Again he returned home, only to resume battling with his father. Things became so serious that the older Haarmann forced Fritz to undergo psychiatric treatment, during which he was diagnosed as a psychopath, deficient in intelligence, unable to comprehend the concept of morality, selfish, vengeful, and inclined to violent behavior. However, there were no medical or legal grounds to confine him for further mental treatment.

His army service earned him a small pension, but he had neither the skills nor the inclination to engage in any socially useful activities. Thus over the next twenty years he spent a third of his life in prison for every possible offense, from fraud and burglary to petty larceny and morals charges.

It was easy for Haarmann to drift into the twilight zone of Hanover's underworld. Occasionally he got handouts from his family; most of the time, however, he lived like a hobo. He was well known to the police as the kind of petty criminal who, when arrested, could be counted on to surrender meekly

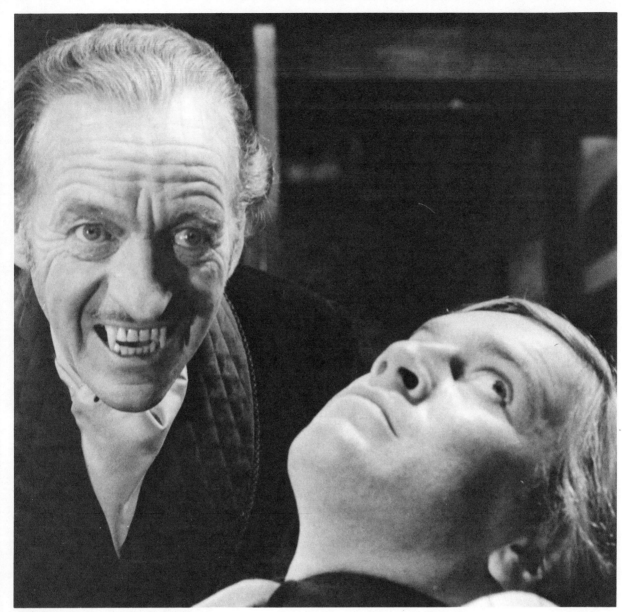

David Niven as an urbane and elegant
Count Dracula in the 1973 film,
Vampira.

without any trouble. In the year 1914 he was sentenced to four years in prison, thus avoiding military service during the First World War.

He found his place in the sewer of society after his release from prison. Rampant inflation raged throughout Germany. There was political chaos, and widespread demoralization swept the country in the wake of defeat. The morale of honest men and women had reached its nadir and only habitues of the gutter thrived. Black marketeers, con men, fences, pimps, and thieves preyed upon whatever victims they could find and grew fat.

Now nearly forty years of age, Haarmann achieved a degree of affluence that he had never before known in his life. Swindling, cheating, smuggling, and stealing, he accumulated enough money to find his own lodgings at 27 Kellerstrasse, in the old section of Hanover. His specialty was black marketeering and resale of stolen clothes. He supplemented his income by turning stool pigeon. Short of funds like everyone else in Germany at that time, the police could not pay informers in cash, so they did the next best thing by offering all petty criminals who cooperated valuable fringe benefits. Taking advantage of the situation to its fullest, Fritz soon acquired the nickname of "Detective Haarmann," and at the same time earned a rather unique status. Having neither scruples nor loyalties, he had no compunctions about turning anyone in if he stood to gain by it; consequently his fellow criminals treated him with an exaggerated degree of respect as insurance against his fingering them. It was bad business to offend "Detective Haarmann." The police, always eager to get the goods whenever and on whomever they wanted, were similarly accommodating. Furthermore, since he always had a steady supply of merchandise, he flourished by underselling his competition.

There was another factor which added to his growing self-satisfaction. Conditions in Germany being what they were, a steady stream of teenage runaways kept flowing into the cities from rural areas where there was little chance of earning a living. Since Haarmann's sexual tastes ran toward handsome teenage boys, he was in his glory. Night after night he would march arrogantly through the local railway station, selecting those who appealed most to his warped tastes. Approaching them with an air of self-assurance he implied that he had some official status. Those he fancied he took home, offering them food and lodging.

Those unfortunate enough to be selected by Haarmaan were as good as dead. His sexual desires were not easily satisfied. When aroused he became homicidal, and he slaked his bloodthirsty appetites by ripping out his victims' throats with his teeth and drinking their blood until he was gorged.

In 1918 he was arrested on a morals charge because of an encounter with a teenager who was fortunate enough to survive. After nine months in jail Haarmann was released, at which time he moved, and in 1919 he took a lover named Hans Grans, a good-looking, twenty-four-year-old petty criminal and male prostitute.

Before long Grans became almost a Svengali to Haarmann. In the course of their sordid liaison he proved the more cold-blooded of the pair. Not only did he select many of the victims, he incited Haarmann to his bloody slayings. While Grans fingered candidates for slaughter, fat Fritz Haarmann wielded the butcher knife, hatchet, and fang.

In the Hammer/Rank Vampire Circus, *1971, Count Mitterhouse, played by Robert Tayman, bares his fangs in anticipation of some fresh young blood.*

On May 17, 1924, the final curtain rose on Fritz Haarmann's bloody drama. Two young boys playing on the banks of the Leine River found a human skull and turned it over to the police. Five days later another skull, somewhat smaller in size, was found further downriver, and on June 13 two more turned up. With an unbelievable lack of concern the police surgeon did not subject the skulls to the required pathological tests. Instead he treated the matter as a grisly practical joke played by some imaginative medical students with a morbid sense of humor. On July 24, however, still another group of boys found a whole sack of human bones, including another skull.

Rumors swiftly spread throughout Hanover. The superstitious whispered about a werewolf, the pragmatic gave convincing arguments in favor of a local Jack the Ripper. Children were locked in after dark by frightened parents and the press began to publish chilling statistics that in the year 1924 alone somewhere around six hundred boys between the ages of fourteen and eighteen had vanished without a trace. Morbid curiosity seekers began gathering on the banks of the river until finally the police decided to make a concerted effort to solve the mystery of the bones. The river was dragged and over five hundred more human bones were recovered. Pathology revealed that they had come from approximately twenty-two bodies of different young men and boys.

By pure coincidence Haarmann was arrested about this time for "committing an indecent act in public." As a routine matter the police searched his quarters and found the place spattered with bloodstains. Initially this aroused no suspicion, for it was known to them that their prisoner was, among other things, engaged in illegal butchering and black marketeering of meat. Another rumor now began to circulate that he was grinding up human flesh and selling it as sausages. Under the circumstances it was only logical that he would come under suspicion as the mysterious boy-killer. He was not talking, however, and the police had no concrete evidence against him. An unexpected break in the case came when the mother of a missing runaway identified a piece of clothing on a stranger as having belonged to her son. When the garment was traced to Haarmann the police lost patience and gave him a going-over of the sort later made infamous by the Gestapo. He broke under the interrogation and confessed.

At his trial the ludicrous-looking, moon-faced vampire was only convicted of murdering twenty-four youths. However, when questioned directly as to how many he had actually killed, he replied, "Thirty or forty, I don't remember exactly." The sensational trial made international headlines and Fritz Haarmann ended up receiving the death penalty. Hans Grans received life in prison. After sentence was pronounced, basking in the glare of his notoriety, Haarmann stood up in court and said in a squeaky, trembling voice, "I want to be executed in the market place. On my tombstone you must put the inscription, 'Here lies mass-murderer Haarmann.' And on my birthday, Hans Grans must come and lay a wreath on it."

It is doubtful if anyone was touched by this ridiculous statement, including Grans, who sat stone-faced through the entire proceedings contemplating his blubbery lover with a contemptuous sneer.

Fritz Haarmann, the Hanover vampire, was executed by decapitation on April 15, 1925.

Peter Kurten—The Düsseldorf Vampire

One night in the 1920s a figure skulked through the darkened Hofgarten, Düsseldorf's Central Park, and sneaked up on a slumbering swan, hacked off its head, and drank up all the blood. Horrible as it sounds, this act was one of the vampire's minor atrocities. This bizarre act was committed by Peter Kurten, the Düsseldorf vampire, known as the Düsseldorf Ripper. Nowhere in the annals of murder is there a case quite like his. Unlike most of his infamous predecessors such as Fritz Haarmann, Kurten's career of savagery and murder followed no precise pattern. For example, Landru-Bluebeard killed only women. Haarmann slaughtered only young men. But Peter Kurten vented his lust for blood on the nation at large, attacking men, women, children, and even animals.

He inspired such revulsion and horror in all of pre-Hitler Germany that filmmaker Fritz Lang made a motion picture based on his career. The film, *M*, turned out to be a classic, and launched a young and relatively unknown actor, Peter Lorre, on a long, succesful international career.

Peter Kurten was an archetypal nonentity. Of medium height, he was a meticulous dresser. The suits, shirts, and neckties he wore were always spotless and well pressed. His neatly combed hair, slightly graying at the temples, gave him the look of a professional man. He frequently heightened this impression by affecting horn-rimmed glasses. Although he never worked at anything more specialized than factory labor, he delighted in passing himself off as an engineer or lower-echelon civil servant. Aside from a tiny, Hitler-type moustache, Kurten was always clean-shaven. Even the cold, fishy eyes and the thin, slightly turned-down mouth gave no hint of the bloodthirsty vampire lurking behind the expresionless facade. A casual pedestrian passing Kurten as he went forth on one of his lethal evening forays would probably never have taken a second look. Yet, to quote Margaret Seaton Wagner's *The Monster of Düsseldorf,* which covered the case thoroughly, "The most extraordinary and horrible thing about Kurten's nocturnal prowling lay in the association with the vampire and the werewolf of ancient tradition. It was his habit and his principal satisfaction to receive the stream of blood that gushed from his victims' wounds to his mouth."

Born in 1883 at Mülheim on the Rhine, Peter Kurten was one of ten children. His father, a sand-molder by trade, was a drunken brute who frequently beat his wife and children. In one of his typically callous admissions, Kurten told all about his early apprenticeship to murder. The lust for blood was awakened in him when still a small child. The family shared a house with the local dog catcher. Since unclaimed strays were sold for meat, it was the dog catcher's job to slaughter and dress them. Kurten recalled with nostalgia the pleasure he used to derive from watching the helpless creatures as they were put to death. He was a good student too, for when he grew older he applied this previously acquired knowledge to the destruction of small birds and animals, which he turned into a profit through regular sales to the local taxidermists. The butchering of pigs—a chore frequently done at home before the turn of the century—was another activity that thoroughly delighted young Peter. This too made a strong impression on him and provided the inspiration to torture sheep when he was thirteen years old.

He embarked on his career of crime at the ripe old age of nine, when for no particular reason he drowned two of his friends in the Rhine. One had accidentally fallen into the

hurled an axe through her kitchen window. The day after that he threw a large rock into her bedroom on the second floor. Then, less than a week later, he fired five pistol shots at her father. Still not content, Kurten followed that episode with a letter to the girl threatening her life if she continued to spurn him. This was the final straw. The harrassed family complained to the authorities. Kurten was arrested and given his first prison sentence, which lasted four years. One year after his release he was sent to prison again for thirty-four thefts and twelve attempted burglaries. This time he got seven years. What the authorities did not know at the time was that their prisoner was a full-fledged pyromaniac as well, for during his first year of freedom he had succeeded in committing four separate acts of arson.

After his release in May 1912, he went back to his favorite means of earning a living, burglary, petty theft, and fraud. He specialized in robbing small, family-operated taverns, finding Friday and Saturday nights to be the most profitable times to operate. The proprietors were usually so busy attending to customers that they never bothered to worry about what might be taking place on the second floor.

It was during the summer of 1913 that Kurten committed his first truly depraved murder, one that was destined to remain unsolved for seventeen years. In keeping with his habit of robbing small taverns he decided to venture out of Düsseldorf and try his luck in Mülheim, the Cologne suburb where he had been born. Selecting a house on Wolff-strasse, he broke in shortly after 10 P.M. and stealthily groped his way up to the second floor. He found nothing worth stealing and finally ventured into a room near the front of the house. A lighted street lamp outside threw a warm glow into the room, clearly revealing its sleeping occupant. There in the

water and every time he tried to climb back up on the raft Kurten pushed his head under. The second boy jumped in to rescue the first and suffered the same fate. The young murderer had experienced his first kill and found it to his liking.

By the time he was seventeen he had developed a decided interest in girls. One day he lured an eighteen-year-old former schoolmate to the woods and tried to coerce her into submitting to his own special brand of sexual relations. It included strangulation. She thought she was finished with him after managing to wriggle from his grasp and flee to her home, but she was wrong. The next day he left-hand corner of the room, snugly tucked beneath a white feather quilt, was a pretty little girl of ten named Christine Klein. As Kurten regarded the child's peaceful face his heart began to pound wildly. Without hesitating he seized her head with his left hand, simultaneously closing the powerful fingers of his right hand over her throat. After no more than a minute and a half of futile struggling the child lost consciousness. Seeing that his victim has stopped struggling and gone limp, Kurten reached into his pocket, took out a small but razor-sharp knife, and snapped it open with a deft flick of the wrist. Then, once again lifting Christine's head, he slit her throat with a single downward stroke. Trembling in the throes of a violent orgasm, Kurten watched the blood spurt from the wound and drip on the floor beside the bed. He stared in glassy-eyed fascination for about three minutes. Then, completely calmed by the release of tension, he checked thoroughly to make certain there were no bloodstains on his clothes. Tiptoeing to the door, he slipped out, locking it behind him, and left the house the way he had entered it. Completely spent, he returned to his flat in Düsseldorf.

Commenting on the episode years later, Kurten said, "People were talking about it all around me. All this amount of indignation and horror did me good."

In and out of prison until the year 1921, Peter Kurten avoided military service during the First World War, where, ironically, he could have found a "legitimate" outlet for his bestial activities.

That year he got married. Although the woman found him charming, she had no love for him. The only reason she agreed to marry him was that he threatened to kill her if she refused. She was not particularly happy with her husband, but Frau Kurten, who soon found her husband to be an incorrigible womanizer, accepted her plight with resignation, considering it a form of divine punishment for her own past sins. Some years before meeting Kurten, when she was twenty-three, she had fallen in love with a young man who had promised to marry her. On the strength of that promise she relinquished her virginity and when he went back on his word she shot him. For this she served four years in prison. Unlike her husband, she was burdened with a conscience, which bothered her despite the fact that she had paid her debt to society.

It was not until 1929 that Peter Kurten embarked on the spectacular series of murders and assaults which ultimately led to his downfall. Between the years 1923 and 1929 he committed seven strangulations and twenty acts of arson upon houses, farms, barns, hayracks, and wagons. Once he even started a whole forest fire. But all these were just preliminaries.

Kurten began his real reign of terror in Düsseldorf on February 3, 1929. It was a Sunday night. A certain Frau Kuhn, on her way home from visiting friends, was just about to turn into a lonely side street when she was seized by the coat sleeve from behind by Kurten. "Keep quiet!" he hissed. "Don't say a word!" Before she could scream she felt a blinding pain in the temple, then another and another and another. After that she lost consciousness. Frau Kuhn was fortunate, for though she received twenty-four stab wounds, she recovered. Unfortunately, she could not give the police a single clue as to the identity of her assailant. Five days later he savagely attacked and mutilated eight-year-old Rose Ohliger and attempted to burn her body with kerosene. Had it not been for the cold, damp, February air, the little corpse might have been consumed by flames. After the two vicious crimes an outraged public clamored for police action. Newspapers has-

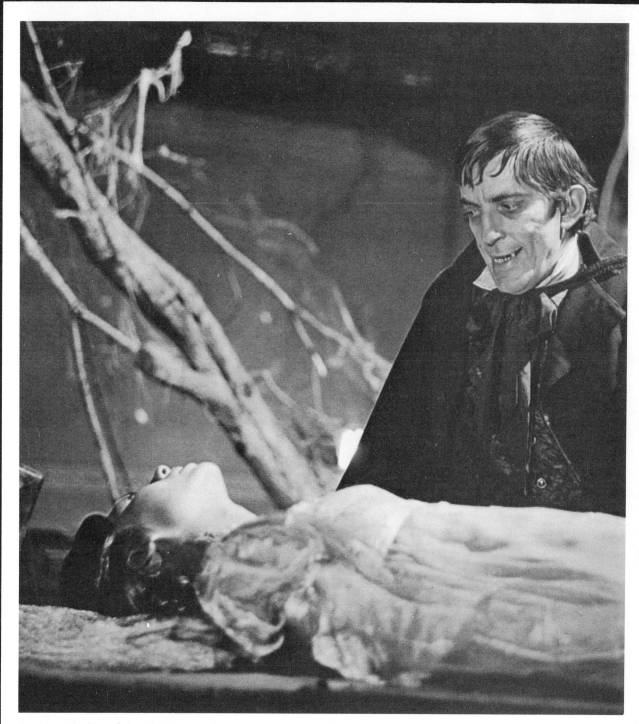

Barnabas Collins of the television soap
Dark Shadows *prepares to take his*
nourishment from a hapless victim.

tened to compare the attacks to England's unsolved Jack the Ripper killings, for like his British counterpart, the Düsseldorf vampire struck without warning and disappeared without a clue. Terror was compounded by confusion, however, because five days later, on February 13, Rudolf Scheer, a forty-five-year-old disabled pensioner, was found dead in the street of the same neighborhood. Like the two earlier victims, Scheer had been brutally stabbed. It was obvious that he had been attacked from behind, receiving multiple stab wounds in the temple. What baffled the police was that Scheer had not been robbed. It was bad enough that the ripper-killer left no clues, but he made matters more difficult by choosing his victims irrespective of age or sex.

In the period between April and July 1929 there were several unsuccessful attacks; then, on July 30, the nude body of a thirty-four-year-old prostitute named Emma Gross was found on a threadbare sofa in a seedy, run-down hotel. She had been stabbed to death. One month later, on the evening of August 29, Kurten struck again, not once but three times. Within the radius of a few blocks all three victims were attacked in a similar manner, stabbed in the back suddenly, without any advance warning. On August 31 there occurred the most shocking murder anyone could remember. Two young girls, aged five and fourteen, were found dead in a suburban bean field. Both children had been strangled, after which their throats had been slashed. Although neither child had been sexually assaulted, both had been savagely and repeatedly stabbed. Kurten's bloody toll for the month of August 1929 alone totaled nine victims. The brutal attacks continued and before long Düsseldorf had acquired the worst reputation in Europe. The mere name of the city was enough to inspire terror. A man in Hungary was actually arrested for mentioning Düsseldorf in a threatening man-

ner. Civilized persons all across the continent became solemn when the city was mentioned and discussed the events there only in subdued tones. Germany now witnessed more concerted police activity than had taken place in decades. The authorities shuddered at each new scare headline. Even the underworld cooperated in the all-out effort to trap the bloody Düsseldorf vampire—professional criminals too drew the line at such horrendous brutality; it gave them a bad name. Extreme measures had become absolutely essential. Journalistic attacks on the police increased each day. Worse yet, the Communist press was stirring up the working classes and the ever-popular Nazi party was creating headaches of another variety.

On November 8, Gertrude Albermann, five years old, was found maimed, pitifully crumpled on a bed of nettles in a rubble-strewn spot near a high brick factory wall. Like most of Kurten's previous victims, the child had been strangled first, then brutally stabbed—in this case, thirty-six times. Taking a cue from his hero, Jack the Ripper, Kurten wrote a letter to the Communist newspaper *Freiheit*. It included a map and explicit directions as to where they might find the body of his latest victim.

Every criminal who is caught eventually makes a fatal mistake that is responsible for ending his career. Peter Kurten's concerned a clever young woman named Maria Büdlick. It was May 14, 1930, and Maria had just arrived in Düsseldorf in search of a new career. It seems strange that a young girl would come alone to a city so associated with deadly terror. But since there had not been a single slaying since November, people were beginning to walk the streets again after dark.

It was late. Maria was pacing up and down the deserted platform of the railway station. A woman who had promised to meet her there had failed to appear. She was wondering what to do next when a strange man approached and asked her what she was doing there alone at that time of night. Maria, fully aware of Düsseldorf's sinister reputation, had no intention of having anything to do with the stranger. He insisted that he knew a respectable hotel nearby and would be glad to show her the way. Again she refused his offer. Just then another man approached and demanded to know what was going on. The first man, looking guilty, stammered out a few platitudes, insisting that his intentions were honorable, then he slunk away into the shadows. Maria Büdlick was not alone with Peter Kurten. Taken in by his outwardly mild manner and respectable appearance, she agreed to accompany him when he volunteered to lead her to a hotel. She even stopped off with him at his flat on Mettmännerstrasse. There he gave her a cup of milk and some bread, but when it became apparent that he had other things on his mind, she demanded to be taken to the hotel. Kurten gave her no argument and instead led her to the Graffenburg woods just northeast of the city. Once they were alone his manner changed. He said, "Now you are alone with me in the woods, you can scream as much as you like. Nobody will hear you." With that he seized her, and with rough, violent motions tried to plant a kiss on her mouth. She fought desperately, straining to turn away her face. One look at her throat was enough for Kurten. Wrapping his hands around her neck he began to strangle her. Then, for reasons known only to himself, he loosened his grip before the girl lost consciousness and asked, "Do you remember where I live?"

"No," lied the terrified Maria, gasping for air. "I'm a stranger here. I only arrived in the city this evening."

At that moment Peter Kurten made the decision that was destined to cost him his head. Assuming that she would be too confused to recognize him again he led her to a well-lighted street where she could find transportation, then turned and left her alone.

Fortunately Maria had an excellent memory. Within twenty-four hours she was leading the police on a street-by-street search for the house of the man who had nearly killed her. When they arrived at 71 Mettmännerstrasse Maria cried out, "That's the house, I'm certain of it."

While questioning the landlady the police noticed, but paid no attention to, a man who passed them on the stairs. Maria started and turned pale. "Was that the man who attacked you?" asked one of the policemen. "Yes," whispered Maria.

"What's his name?" another officer asked the landlady.

"Peter Kurten," she replied. "He and his wife have lived here for years."

It was an important day. The police finally knew the name of the Düsseldorf vampire.

Actually Kurten was not arrested for another ten days. When he recognized Maria Budlick on the stairs that fateful night, he knew that his Götterdämmerung was at hand. Before being arrested he made a complete confession of his crimes to his wife. Bursting into tears the horrified woman threatened to commit suicide if he did not turn himself in. After listening to her husband's pleas, Frau Kurten did something much more sensible. She notified the police herself. For this he bore her no grudge. He even expressed satisfaction that she was able to collect part of the substantial reward that had been posted for his apprehension.

Kurten was amazingly cooperative: once in custody he held nothing back. He said, "Very well, I will confess, but I promise, you are going to hear some very gruesome things."

When Kurten's entire grisly story came out the public was stunned with horror. Not only did the man possess an exceptionally high intelligence, he had an almost photographic memory. With obvious relish he related in detail virtually every depravity he had perpetrated over the years. Throughout he was chillingly calm and extremely accurate. He expressed no regret about the crimes he had committed; yet he had the profound gall to ask the relatives of his victims to forgive him and pray for his soul. To those victims who were still alive he offered his most profound and courteous apologies; but he confided to the police, "If I were outside again today I couldn't guarantee that something of the kind might not happen again. I haven't felt any pricks of conscience up to now. I could not act differently."

The predominant theme running through his confession was his preoccupation with blood. Every time he described a murder he would make such statements as "I saw the blood flowing," or "I heard the blood gush out," or "she lost a great deal of blood." He said that the most powerful sexual stimulant for him was the sight and sound of dripping blood, and he admitted to drinking it as often as he could.

The date for his execution was set for 6:00 A.M. on July 2, 1931, after a sensational trial. According to ritual the condemned man was given his choice of a last meal. He selected Wiener schnitzel, potatoes, vegetables, and white wine. He enjoyed the food so much he ordered seconds of everything. When the dishes were cleared away a deep calm settled over him. He had such presence of mind that he speculated with one of the guards whether or not a man who had been guillotined would remain conscious long enough to be aware of the sound of his own blood spurting from his neck after his head had been chopped off.

So it was that Kurten went off to join his victims, receiving in the process "a short, sharp shock" from a blade larger and keener than any he had ever wielded himself. It is just as well that we will never learn the answer to his last question.

A vampire, having metamorphosed into a bat, soars over the graveyard and off into the night in search of victims.

The Kensington Vampire

Certainly one of the most publicized vampire-killers to emerge after the Second World War was a rather mild-looking Englishman named John George Haigh. Though he was not as spectacular or melodramatic as Dracula, Haigh's career was as gruesome as that of any of his blood-drinking predecessors. Since he preyed upon twentieth-century victims, however, his career was terminated at the end of a rope rather than by a stake through the heart.

Born in 1910, Haigh was raised by rigidly fundamentalist parents belonging to a strict religious sect known as the Pilgrim Brethren. From childhood on Haigh lived in an environment of repressive religious fanaticism.

All worldly pleasures were absolutely forbidden. Not only did the list of prohibitions include the obvious ones, such as dancing, gambling, liquor, and the theater, but even the daily papers were proscribed.

As a young boy John was discouraged from associating with other children. He was forbidden to bring any schoolmates home. There was only one goal toward which he had to strive at all times and that was heavenly salvation. The only way for him to achieve it was by "the blood of the heavenly lamb." The only God he knew was a vengeful, angry deity with boundless wrath, who punished earthly transgressors with eternal damnation.

To make matters worse, Haigh's mother was a superstitious, ignorant woman who in-

Medieval drawing of tormented souls in Hell, the sort of imagery that would have been impressed on John George Haigh as a boy.

stilled in him the worst of her mediocre beliefs, fears, and guilts. She firmly believed that dreams foretold the future. As a result, when John began to have fearful nightmares of Christ slowly bleeding to death on the cross he developed severe anxieties. The very thought of his Savior dying so painfully and slowly afflicted him in a multitude of ways. The most significant of these was that when he committed murder he made it a point to do away with his victims painlessly and quickly.

His recurrent dreams of the bleeding Christ continued with relentless regularity until he reached the age of sixteen. This caused him to spend many agonized hours of his free time asking himself why poor Jesus had been permitted to suffer so. When the dreams finally stopped and he was old enough to make his own decisions, he chose to leave the Pilgrim Brethren and joined the Church of England. He became a choirboy and eventually an assistant organist. At age seventeen he won a prize for writing an essay titled "St. Peter in the Gospels and in the Acts." It was about this time that he experienced what he described at his trial as his first "divine revelation." The revelation, he declared, consisted of instructions from heaven to drink his own urine. This most likely stemmed from a twisted interpretation of the Scriptures he had come to know so well. For in Proverbs V:15 there is a passage saying "Drink water out of thine own cistern and running waters out of thine own well." And in John VII:38, "He that believeth in me, as the Scriptures hath said, out of his belly shall flow rivers of living water."

Dreadful nightmares that began afflicting Haigh after he became an adult eventually impelled him to become a modern-day vampire. The dreams began in 1944 and in retrospect gave psychiatrists a keen insight into the disordered mind that had produced them. In each dream Haigh entered a forest of crucifixes which was slowly transformed into trees with twisted branches dripping with human blood. Always one of the trees would undergo a metamorphosis into the shape of a man, who collected a bowlful of blood from another tree. As the blood dripped into the bowl the tree became pale, and Haigh felt himself grow weaker. The man then held forth the bowl and invited Haigh to drink the blood. He knew that this was the only way for him to regain his strength, but every time he reached out the figure of the man would recede and fade. The dreams always ended before he could reach the man and obtain the blood. He would then awaken in a state of agitation and deep anxiety. Haigh discovered that the only way to prevent the man from fading away, so that he could seize the proffered bowl and drink the blood, was to kill someone during his waking hours and drink the victim's blood. He was so expert at seeking out and slaying victims that he did not even come under police suspicion until after he had successfully done away with his ninth, a sixty-nine-year-old widow, Mrs. Olivia Ellen Henrietta Olive Roberts Durand-Deacon.

Haigh first met Mrs. Durand-Deacon while both resided at the Onslow Court Hotel in South Kensington, London. Haigh was the director of a small firm called Hurstlea Products, Ltd. It did not, however, provide him with a steady income. The most significant aspect of his connection with the firm was that it gave him access to a storehouse in a small shed in a construction yard on Leopold Road in Crawley.

Haigh insinuated his way into his last victim's confidence one evening in the hotel dining room. He told her that he had invented a new process for manufacturing artificial fingernails. She displayed an im-

A Life: Dreams, by Max Klinger.

mediate interest and he offered to take her to his "laboratory," where she might see the process for herself.

On February 18, 1949, he met Mrs. Durand-Deacon in the lobby of the hotel, drove her to Crawley, and invited her into the darkened storehouse. Then, as she waited patiently to see what she was expecting, Haigh calmly withdrew a .38-calibre Enfield revolver and shot her in the head. It was what happened next that shocked all of England when the story broke in the press. Said Haigh later when he confessed, "I went out and fetched a drinking glass, and made an incision in the side of her neck, and collected a glass of blood which I drank."

When that was done he carefully removed all of her clothes and jewelry, dragged the body to a forty-five-gallon tank, and dumped it in. Next he poured thirty-five gallons of sulfuric acid in, stirring it well to make sure that no part of the corpse was protected from the corrosive liquid. When satisfied that he had succeeded in his efforts he turned out the light, locked the door as he left, and went to a small nearby restaurant for tea.

Some hours later, after tea, he returned to the shed, took a pump and added more acid to the tank. By now he had worked up another appetite, so he went to the Hotel George in Crawley, had dinner, then returned to his lodgings in South Kensington. He made a foolish mistake the next day. He took Mrs. Durand-Deacon's watch, pawned her jewelry, and took her fur coat to a dry cleaner.

On February 21 one of Mrs. Durand-Deacon's friends, concerned over not having seen her for a few days, approached Haigh and suggested that the two of them report her disappearance to the police. The accommodating vampire seemed more than happy to comply with her request. First, however, he returned to the scene of the crime in Crawley to check the vat. He wanted to be certain that the body had completely dissolved. Part of it remained, so after pouring off some of the sludge and adding more acid, he returned to South Kensington and went to the police, expressing concern about the missing Mrs. Durand-Deacon. They were suspicious of him and decided to check him out. What he had no way of knowing was that they very quickly traced his victim's pawned jewelry to him. Meanwhile, the following day, on February 22, Haigh went back to Crawley to look into the vat of acid again. The body had by now completely dissolved. Curiously, a plastic handbag was still relatively intact. Consequently, after dumping out the remaining sludge he disposed of the handbag.

On February 26 Haigh was summoned by the police and confronted with the evidence that they had gathered. He admitted knowing about the jewelry and declared that to explain the matter fully would necessitate his implicating many people, that the affair was much too complicated. Finally he told his interrogators, "If I told you the truth you wouldn't believe me. It sounds too fantastic for belief."

Haigh was then told that anything further he said might be held against him, but he impatiently replied, "I understand all that. Mrs. Durand-Deacon no longer exists. She has disappeared completely and no trace of her can ever be found. I've destroyed her with acid. You'll find the sludge that remains at Leopold Road. I did the same with the Hendersons and the McSwanns. Every trace has gone. How can you prove murder if there's no body?"

What Haigh did not realize was that a body is not necessarily required to establish a

*Vampire Miriam, played by actress
Anulka, attacks one of her victims in the
Fox-Rank film,* Vampyres.

homicide. Not only had he confessed to the slaying of Mrs. Durand-Deacon, he had admitted other murders that were not even on the books. Coming to the conclusion that they were probably dealing with a madman trying to call attention to himself, the police asked him to make an official statement which would be transcribed for the record. This he readily agreed to do and when the stenographer was ready he began to talk.

During the course of his confession, in describing each of the killings, he used such phrases as "I hit him on the head with a cosh, withdrew a glass of blood as before and drank it," or, "I tapped her on the head with a cosh and tapped her for blood."

It occurred to the police that Haigh's calm admissions to being a vampire-killer might well serve a double purpose. He might very likely be preparing the way for a defense on the grounds of insanity. A full-scale investigation was launched. A team of lab experts from Scotland Yard went out to Crawley and gathered samples of the sludge. According to Police Commissioner Sir Harold Scott, the findings included "the handle of a red plastic handbag, some false teeth, three gallstones, some fragments of human bone, and a mass of yellow substance resembling melted body fat. Examinations of the gallstones showed them to be of the human type; the bones, too, were human and probably those of an elderly woman . . . the teeth were identified by the dentist who had supplied them to Mrs. Durand-Deacon."

There was much more damning evidence, all of which pointed at John George Haigh. He was then formally charged with murder and placed under arrest. Had it not been for stringent British laws against excessive pretrial publicity in such cases, the press would have had a field day with sensational headlines and vampire-killer stories. There were nonetheless a number of such stories, resulting in the arrest of one publisher who received a three-month prison sentence for contempt of court.

The trial did not take place until the following July, but when it opened at the Sussex Assizes, on High Street, thousands of morbidly curious spectators swarmed in the streets. They did not intend to be deprived of the opportunity to catch a glimpse of a real-life vampire.

Although the prosecution had thirty witnesses, there was only one testifying for the defense, psychiatrist Dr. Harvey Yellowlees. Throughout the trial Haigh remained calm and composed. The *Times* (London) reported that he was "callous, cheerful, and blandly indifferent as he confessed." Only once during the entire trial did he ever become upset. This was when the slayings were referred to as murders. He objected strenuously to the term, maintaining that it was his destiny to commit them, and that they were purely ritual in nature. There was no question of right or wrong, he explained. To the end he insisted that each killing came about as a result of divine revelation. Furthermore, he declared vaguely that his drinking of blood was related in some abstract way to eternal life. Perhaps he entertained thoughts of being a real vampire.

The defense was unable to prove insanity in the legal sense, largely because of two strong technical points introduced by the prosecution. According to the McNaughton Rules, which contained the standards by which an individual was to be acquitted of murder by reason of insanity, the accused was not considered legally insane if he knew "the nature and quality of his act." Haigh was fully aware at all times of what he had

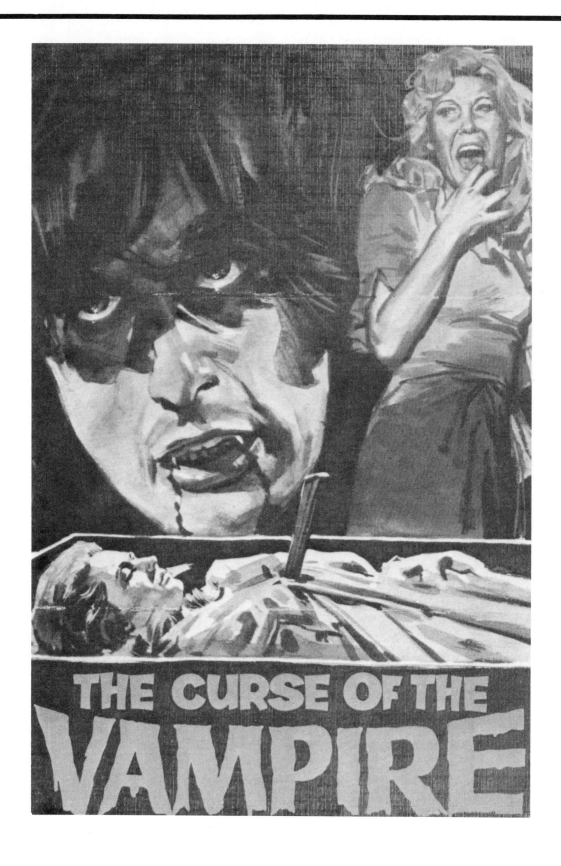

Typical lurid vampire film poster.

done. Besides, he had accumulated a substantial profit along the way. John George Haigh was finally convicted and sentenced to hang, thus ringing down the curtain on one of the most bizarre vampire cases in postwar England.

Other Contemporary Vampires

The preceding accounts deal with only a handful of the most celebrated—or, if you will, the most notorious—cases of actual, living vampires. But there are many more, all over the world, that continually make sensational newspaper copy. The following brief examples are only a sampling of what can be found if one makes a serious effort to keep score.

The *Fortean Times*, a publication devoted to strange happenings, reported the case of a woman who, significantly enough, called herself Lilith. She met a young man in a cemetery one night and apparently inspired him to become amorous. He attempted to kiss her, but suddenly she sank her teeth into his neck and held him down with an "unnatural surge of strength" until she had drawn blood. When questioned she admitted to having attacked a number of people in a similar manner, although she did not refer to herself as a vampire. Instead she said that she was "a very evil person who liked the taste of blood. I just like being evil." She had also been involved in a witch coven, but when someone suggested that she use her own father as a blood sacrifice she drew the line.

A contemporary vampire from Rhode Island named Carl Johnson was described as having first developed a taste for blood after

creeping into the bedroom of his sleeping sister, whereupon he punctured her leg and sucked her blood. After that he organized a satanic cult and asserted that when he sucked the blood of a victim he could feel himself becoming physically stronger. It has been reported, however, that since then he has been "cured" and has gone on the lecture circuit to describe his experiences as a vampire.

In Nuremberg, West Germany, a forty-one-year-old deaf mute named Kuno Hofmann was arrested for vampirism. He confessed to having dug up approximately thirty freshly buried women in fifteen cemeteries around Germany, for the purpose of drinking their blood. This assertion is subject to question, however, for if the bodies were embalmed there would be no blood left. In May 1972 he shot a couple sleeping in a parked car and drank the blood from their head wounds. He also attempted on more than one occasion to break into undertakers' establishments. Once he tried to murder a mortuary attendant who apprehended him in the act of searching for bodies. In a statement to the police he said, "I drank the blood of the women because I wanted to feel it in my body. I need a liter of women's blood every day. I've got used to it now." During his trial in August 1974, it was revealed that Hofmann had spent nineteen out of the past twenty-four years in mental institutions and prisons. Shades of Peter Kurten.

In 1975, a woman named Bahya Lenpeng, a twenty-five-year-old Indonesian from a small Sumatran village, proved to be a particularly vicious vampire. Over a period of two years she married six husbands and succeeded in killing five. Like the black widow spider, she commenced her lethal assaults on the wedding night. Her method was simple. After giving her unwitting bridegrooms a powerful sleeping potion, she would make a

A determined, sexy vampire on the attack in the 1970 Hammer film, Vampire Lovers.

small incision in an artery and start drinking blood while the man was unconscious. Not a single one of the first five husbands suspected a thing and each died of anemia within a month of the first vampire attack. It was with the sixth husband that she made the error that proved her undoing. He was a local policeman and instead of drinking the drugged tea she offered, he pretended to fall asleep. Then, when she attempted to drink his blood, he jumped out of bed, handcuffed her, and took her off to jail. She was tried, convicted, and given a suspended sentence for manslaughter.

In 1975 English newspapers reported that a nine-year-old child named Tracy Robson, of Essex, was attacked by a masked man who leaped from the bushes, bit the girl on the cheek, and ran off licking the blood from his lips. He was never apprehended.

In June 1979, twenty-eight-year-old Richard T. Chase was convicted of murder in Palo Alto, California. He had killed six residents of Sacramento, including a pregnant woman and an infant, in December 1977 and January 1978. In each case he multilated the corpses of his victims for the express purpose of drinking their blood. He told the court-appointed psychiatrist that he required human blood in order to deal with his own physical ailments.

In view of the horror associated with so many of the living vampires in our midst, it may seem strange that there are many vampires of a benign nature who have no desire to harm or bring pain to the persons they seek out to supply them with the blood they require. One such, a woman living in a suburb of New York, is an outstanding example. Of East European extraction, she grew up in a home where many of the old death customs were observed. At the demise of a close relative, she reported, mirrors were covered up while the body lay in the coffin in the parlor because it was feared that the image of the deceased might get trapped in the mirror and find no rest, thus causing the deceased to become a vampire after death. In addition, the windows and doors were sealed shut to prevent any small animal from entering the house and creeping under the coffin or jumping over it, for that too, her family believed, would result in the dead person's post-mortem transition from lifeless corpse to true, undead vampire.

While teaching school she frequently had to deal with children who had cut or scraped themselves during recess. Whenever this occurred she would blot the blood with absorbent tissue, and one day she inadvertently tasted fresh blood. A strange sense of exhilaration came over her and she tried it again. Soon she found herself taking more and more blood, always that which she had soaked up in a tissue. The craving grew stronger and she began to ask herself what was causing this strange thirst for blood.

On reflection she said, "From the age of twelve I was always interested in the occult and the supernatural. I began reading comic books about vampires and werewolves, ghosts and witches. But the vampire legends struck me in particular—the way they had hypnotic control over their victims—generally speaking, a great deal of power. And that was something I did not have as a twelve-year-old child."

An abused child, she was beaten and ridiculed by the relatives who were bringing her up. Her sense of impotence grew stronger, and she would take refuge in her fantasies. Recalling her early experiences of tasting blood, she said, "A feeling of warmth and happiness would come over me." During the entire time she taught school this was the way she obtained blood.

Then she left her teaching job. She became a clerk in a shop and devised a ruse for getting blood. "I would ask my fellow salesgirls if they would like me to do a good luck charm for them, and I would burn a lucky candle for them, selecting a different color according to their desires—pink for friendship, green for good health, gold for money. I told them that I would do this in exchange for three drops of blood, but they never knew what I was really doing with the blood. They would give it to me on a piece of paper and I would take it home and eat it from the paper."

Some time after that she met another woman with a similar taste for blood. They became fast friends. The other woman, somewhat younger, had developed a similar fascination for vampirism, and in the course of her schooling had met someone who had provided her with medical lancets, small sharp metal objects used by doctors for taking blood samples from the fingers. Now the mild-mannered vampire began drinking fresh blood. It became a mutual affair: the two friends took blood from one another and shared it. The older woman then began feeling a sexual attraction for the younger one that was enhanced by the consumption of her blood. They would lie together in a strong embrace, drinking one another's blood.

Giggling in a manner most unexpected in a vampire, she admitted that she would like to draw some blood by biting her friend in the neck but as her teeth were not sharp enough she would never seriously consider it. Then, assuming a somber expression, she said, "I've had nightmares about turning into a vampire and flying high over the treetops with the full moon beaming down. Then I would swoop down on my victims and rip their throats out. But it was strictly a dream. I've never wanted to harm people in real life." When she was asked point-blank if she would bite people in the neck and drink their blood with their consent, she nodded affirmatively, but qualified the statement by adding that she was not necessarily restricted to the neck. If given permission, she would bite the person on any part of the anatomy she or he requested.

The Sangroids

Although it is a little-known fact, contemporary vampires prefer to refer to themselves as Sangroids. They are not yet quite ready to "go public," but unlike their predecessors of past centuries, they are very concerned about their image. They have a difficult task ahead of them because they must overcome centuries of prejudice and fear in order to integrate themselves into contemporary society. Fortunately, through the assistance of ordinary human beings who know of their plight and are actively concerned with their well-being, a major breakthrough is at hand.

Possibly the first person ever to openly come forth and speak about them, for the purpose of promoting better understanding, is Monica Mobley of Louisville, Kentucky. Like so many individuals throughout the world, Ms. Mobley became fascinated with the subject of vampirism as a child. "I was taken to see scary pictures when I was little," she declared. "And I liked the vampire motif. From the cinema I began exploring the literature. In 1971 I started teaching literature and cinema at the University of Louisville. The outcropping of this was that people began coming to me and saying, 'Hey, you really know what you're talking about. I need help. I drink blood, but I don't want to hurt people. I hate myself for it, but I can't help myself. Can you help me?' I soon discovered that a number of people who had been hanging around me and didn't mind my own 'weirdness' were actually Sangroids, which is what they prefer to be called."

She went on to explain that they are in touch with each other and form a decided subculture. "It is almost like a secret lodge," she said. "There are good as well as bad in the group. They are all over the world in just infinite varieties. I had all sorts of requests, from 'Can I have some of your blood?' to 'How can I get blood without hurting people?'"

Now fascinated beyond anything that had ever presented itself to her before, she began working closely with Sangroids, saying, "We actually had workshops featuring biting techniques. I never advocated it, but on the other hand, I accept them. If someone comes to me and says, 'I have to drink blood to survive,' then I don't say, 'Oh, my God! That's disgusting.' I don't have the right to throw stones at anyone."

The matter of the strength of their need for blood arose and she said, "There are those who need it to exist. Then there are others who require it less frequently, depending on whether they are of the human or nonhuman variety." As to how they became vampires, she explained, "Some of them were born that way. There are diseases like porphyria that everyone knows about. But there are two theories. One is the evolutionary theory that some people carry genes that are atavistic, that have vampiristic traits. Then there is the theory that perhaps the condition is due to something alien, some extraterrestrial interference with human women."

One of her most startling revelations about vampires was the explanation of how the aging process affects them: "They reach their prime of physical attractiveness and after that they do not age. That is it. For example, I know a gentleman who claims to be well over five hundred years old, and his credentials are quite substantial. Originally he came from India."

Monica Mobley was asked to elaborate on how they specifically obtained blood from living humans, and replied that they did not do so by biting *per se*. "Are you familiar with 'hickeys'?" she asked, with a chuckle. "After the skin is made supple by sucking on it the teeth can be pressed into it so that blood is drawn without actually biting. After all, biting could be fatal. If you hit the carotid artery then the person would be gone in three minutes. Besides, no one has teeth sharp enough, and let's face it, the teeth part of it isn't what's fun."

As to the specific amount of blood they require, she explained: "That varies with age. The average is from three to six ounces per day, the six ounces being for someone who has really been around for a long time." In an emergency, could they survive on

Somehow, John Carradine makes a very unconvincing Dracula in the 1945 Universal potboiler, House of Dracula, *which also starred Lon Chaney, Jr. (not shown here).*

plasma? "Oh yes, but it's not as decent. It's okay, but it isn't life. It has to do with the metaphysicality of the human spirit, which can't be put into a little plastic vial."

A logical question to ask Ms. Mobley was whether or not some vampires extracted blood by less direct means, such as a syringe. "Let me clarify that. There are those who lust after blood, but who can survive without it. They are not necessarily pleasure seekers. They really need the blood in their diet, but they can get by with as little as a few ounces a year. Now the Sangroids have to have it on a regular basis, and I have found in my experience that if they go without much more than six days they start deteriorating."

Anyone familar with the better-known vampire fiction knows that vampires are supposed to be fatally allergic to sunlight. Not so, asserted Ms. Mobley. "This depends on the condition of the body. There are those who are allergic to sunlight, but there are also those who soak it up and get charged like batteries."

One of the most intriguing aspects of the vampire's existence today was that of how they obtained their blood without doing injury to anyone. She described persons—ordinary humans—whom she referred to as "professional donors," explaining that there are "several undercover establishments where people can be immunized, so if they have partners whom they supply they cannot become infected with vampirism, which can be contagious. It is spread by something like a virus. It isn't a hit-or-miss situation. The donors must take courses on how to give blood and both parties have to take these courses. The donors have iron therapy, they are weighed; if their blood pressure is down or too high, then they're not allowed to participate in the program. But there are those who don't adhere to the safer proceedures.

So there's a black market—or a 'red market,' as it were—people who go out and give blood here and there, but they usually pay a high price in the long run."

There have been a number of allegations of certain vampires ingesting animal blood. She knew of some instances that had occurred in the Louisville area, specifically in a district called Crestwood, where cows were found bloodless under circumstances that indicated the blood had been removed by individuals who apparently were medically proficient. She compared those vampires who have a preference for animal blood to the Masai of Africa, who drink blood mixed with milk as a regular part of their diet.

What undoubtedly proved to be Ms. Mobley's most startling piece of information was her admission that she herself supplies blood on a regular basis to a male vampire with whom she enjoys a close personal relationship." It's a romantic kind of thing," she explained, adding that she permits him to have blood every six days. "He is a true undead," she went on to say, "and he has a soporific substance in his saliva so that there is no pain involved, in fact it is a very pleasurable experience. And there's no danger as long as I take good care of myself and we don't get too carried away. . . . He claims to be seven hundred and six years old, but he can't verify much more than ninety years. He looks about twenty-seven, he's five-ten and weighs one hundred and fifty-five pounds, and comes from Egypt originally." It was impossible to obtain a photograph of him. "He doesn't photograph, unfortunately," Ms. Mobley apologized, adding that he casts no reflection in mirrors either because he is "soulless."

She was anxious to clarify several other points about vampires, shattering a few misconceptions in the process. "This business

Arte Johnson as a bumbling Renfield plays sidekick to a hip Count Dracula, played by George Hamilton with a Bela Lugosi accent, in the hilarious spoof, Love at First Bite.

about bats," she said. "Most of it is hypnosis. They can put you under and make you think you saw them appear as a bat or a mist. But usually he can just snap his fingers and be exactly where he wants to be by means of teleportation." That would unquestionably explain why there have been so many accounts of vampires appearing and disappearing so suddenly.

Ms. Mobley wanted to present the vampire attitude toward some of these misconceptions about them, pointing out that the old belief that they could not bear the sight of crucifixes was sheer nonsense, adding that many of them are extremely religious. Most, she said, live relatively ordinary lives, pursuing such mundane occupations as insurance sales and independent business. "You might even run into one at a Jehovah's Witness meeting," she declared. "They're just everyday people like the rest of us except that they have special dietary needs. For the most part they are harmless, just as the average American citizen is harmless. It's just that the nonharmless ones get all the press coverage."

Most vampires, declared Ms. Mobley, deplore the fact that the general public takes the subject of vampirism so seriously. "I've never met one of them who didn't have a sense of humor," she said. "For example, they just loved George Hamilton's *Love at First Bite.* They're so tired of being depicted as the heavies. For example, Barnabas Collins was okay, but he was one-dimensional— 'Oh, my God! I need blood but I don't want to take it. . . . Oops! here I go again, I'm going to have to bite somebody.' They are so tired of that. If a person is Catholic and you see a play about them you may or may not hear about it, but if it's about vampires a big deal is made about it."

On the subject of an ABC television sitcom about a family of vampires emigrating to the Bronx, she chuckled and expressed the opinion that any vampires going there would have a hard time surviving. "It's the real people out there," she observed, "that make vampires look like angels." Ms. Mobley emphasized that she was not attempting in any way to "seduce" anyone into becoming a vampire, especially as she has written two books on the subject. One, in the lighter vein, is *How to Become a Vampire in Thirty Days—a Practical Guide,* and the other is *A Victim's Chronicle.* "All I want to do," she insisted, "is help people."

Count Krolock, lying helpless in his coffin on the verge of being staked, in Roman Polanski's 1967 film, Dance of the Vampires.

Frank Langella in his portrayal of Dracula as sex object, in Universal Pictures' 1979 remake of the 1931 classic.

Chapter 5

THE PHYSIOLOGY OF THE VAMPIRE

The following is a translation of a paper delivered by Professor Feodor Stepanovich Andreiev of the Soviet Institute of Esoteric Studies in Kiev. Little is known about the institute because the Russians are sensitive about the attitudes of Western social scientists toward subjects regarded to be outside the boundaries of conventional studies. A transcript was made in shorthand of Professor Andreiev's address by a dissident graduate student who slipped it to a sympathetic Czech journalist who, in turn, passed it to a CIA case officer in Prague. When it was translated by Central Intelligence experts in Washington, the text was officially declared to be of no value to American security and was declassified. It was eventually ordered to be destroyed in the late 1970s, when substantial quantities of information were being transferred from paper files to computer. The computer programmer in charge of the task, being an amateur vampirologist, received permission from her superiors to retain it as a curiosity, and she made it available for this book.

Text

From the earliest days of the Socialist Revolution, Marxist social scientists have regarded any studies of antiquated superstitious beliefs as counterproductive. In the old, imperialist days of the czars, it was to the advantage of the ruling classes to strengthen their shackles on the masses by perpetuating a belief system which incorporated saints and angels, devils, demons, ghosts, vampires, and werewolves.

There is an old Russian proverb, however, which states, "Often from the waters of superstition arises the wispy mist of truth." This is not to say that any reputable socialist scientist will devote unnecessary time or effort in pursuit of worthless goals. But it behooves them to investigate anything which may in the long run prove valuable to the state and, in consequence, be of value to the people.

Recent studies, the result of compilations of information gathered since the 1940s, have proved conclusively that the so-called vampire, for so many centuries regarded as a figment of superstitious imaginations, is not only a past and present reality; it is a phenomenon which can, with the necessary checks and balances, be turned eventually into an invaluable asset to the Soviet system.

Yes, dear colleagues, though I hear sniggers among you, I can assure you that vampires are very real, although in no way to be confused with imaginary supernatural monsters.

By way of introduction, let me roll back the time clock of history for a moment to refresh the memories of those among you who have never concerned yourselves with what would in the past quite rightly have been regarded as supersitious myth. What was a vampire in the eyes of our benighted ancestors? He was a vicious, amoral, blood-sucking corpse, reanimated by mysterious means. He lurked in graveyards to attack the living, not only for the purpose of ingesting their blood, but to tear them to pieces and devour their flesh. To be sure, a stupid belief, but one that nonetheless was held to be absolute truth.

I will not waste your valuable time by going into detail in recounting old wives' tales of vampire attacks. I am going to report to you facts that have been thoroughly investigated and are currently under further exhaustive study.

Shortly before the outbreak of World War II, a private in the army was observed by several of his comrades apparently preparing to commit an act of rape upon a young woman in the woods outside of the camp in which they were stationed. Although they attempted to stop him and take him back under arrest, they found him to possess what was termed "superhuman strength." After fling-

ing them about like so many sticks of wood, he apparently vanished without a trace before their eyes. The would-be victim seemed to be in a trance-state, from which she emerged when she was taken to the dispensary. She had not been sexually abused, but there was a small incision on her neck and medical examination proved that she had lost approximately a pint of blood. But there were no bloodstains on her clothing. It was a mystery, and an investigation was launched at once.

The four soldiers were the finest examples of Soviet military men. Two of them recognized the criminal and the others recognized an insignia on his uniform. As a result of their observations the man was quickly found. Because of his great strength it was decided not to attempt to take him by force, but to trick him into submitting to interrogation voluntarily.

He was told by his platoon sergeant that he was being considered for a promotion and had to take a series of tests. The testing officer, of course, was a psychiatrist of such skill that by the end of the interview the man not only admitted what he had done, he pleaded that it was a matter of his survival, that without blood he could not live.

The soldier was a medical orderly and when he said that he drank the blood of patients while they slept, the decision was made to admit him to the Krilov Psychiatric Institute in Leningrad for further examination. He was warned that if he attempted to resist, he would be shot.

For reasons related to internal security, nothing further can be said about the man, his identity, or the specific nature of the special training he was given after a year of physical and mental examinations. It may be stated, however, that the man was what would have been called a vampire in earlier days.

LESSER-KNOWN WAYS OF BECOMING A VAMPIRE

1. *Smoking on holy days.*
2. *Having sexual intercourse with one's grandmother.*
3. *Unclean birds or animals settling on the grave, leaping under a dead body, or creeping under the coffin.*
4. *Having been a wizard during one's life-time.*
5. *Having been a heretic.*
6. *Having been born illegitimate of illegitimate parents (see The Nosferat).*
7. *Having been a werewolf.*
8. *Committing suicide.*
9. *Committing perjury.*
10. *Being buried without proper sacraments.*
11. *Dying unbaptized.*
12. *Dying by violence or drowning.*
13. *Being born with a caul.*
14. *Being born the seventh male or female in a row to the same parents.*
15. *Having chorea.*
16. *Having been born with teeth.*

It is the matter of his peculiar physiology and that of others like him who have been discovered since that time that we may discuss at this time.

As far as we have been able to determine, vampires are a subdivision of genus *homo sapiens* who have existed in our midst for an undetermined period of time. They themselves have no idea as to whether their differences are the result of a mutation millenia ago, or whether they were originally afflicted with a viroid organism which brought about physiological changes which were then carried in their genes, and in some instances transmitted to other humans in the same manner as infectious diseases. These aspects are still under study.

The vampire is essentially physically identical to the ordinary human. The vital organs are the same. Many of the body functions are the same. The body temperature, however, is considerably lower, varying from 28° to 30° Celsius. Similarly, respiration and pulse are far lower and therefore the overall metabolism is much slower. Although the gastrointestinal system resembles that of the ordinary human, it functions differently. For example there is no peristaltic action in the intestinal tract since the vampire does not ingest solid foods. The body is nourished as the ingested blood is absorbed by a process of osmotic action which in turn stimulates endocrine secretions. Depending upon the degree of nourishment the individual is active or lethargic to a greater or lesser degree.

Perhaps the most interesting aspect of the vampire's method of nourishment and digestion is the manner in which the blood is stored. The stomach acts as a reservoir and by means of a valve in the duodonum, which serves as a regulator, a steady supply of blood is released into the intestinal tract, where it is absorbed into the body. If an individual's intake is sufficient enough to fill the stomach to capacity it is possible to go without taking nourishment for as long as five days, just as a camel may go for an extended period of time without drinking water. This would also explain why, in olden times, when a suspected vampire was destroyed by means of driving a stake into the body, blood poured out.

Perhaps the most exciting characteristic of the vampire's body is its cellular structure. There appears to be a rejuvenative factor in the cells which slows down, if not altogether retards, aging. This process is not yet fully understood and is at present undergoing intensive study. A similarly fascinating quality of the vampire's body is the presence of what can only be described as a universal antibody. Not only does this antibody attack and destroy virtually every bacterium and virus that may be introduced, it appears to be anticarcinogenic. And although it has been extracted and used experimentally on cancer patients with little success, oncologists hold forth great hope that a breakthrough in this area may be imminent.

When at the peak of their energy, vampires possess incredible strength, enabling them to move with such great speed as to create the illusion that they have vanished into thin air. Their superior agility also tends to reinforce the impression. Still another aspect of their physical makeup which invariably proves to be advantageous to them is the lack of brittleness in their bones. This permits them to fall or leap from great heights without any particular danger. Their eyesight is also remarkable. Not one who has submitted to physical examination has proved to have a visual acuity of less than 20/20. Furthermore, their ability to see in near-absolute darkness enables us to compare their vision to the electronic light image amplifier.

The genito-urinary system of the male vampire functions not unlike that of the human. We have not studied any females. The penis is erectile. The ejaculatory mechanism is, in fact, identical to that of the average male, although the semen is of a pinkish color. The urine of a vampire has a reddish hue, and the Cowper's glands secrete an amber lubricant which has a consistency and specific gravity approximately the same as safflower oil.

The circulatory system is truly amazing, as is the blood that they produce. The leucocytes contribute to the powerful immune system to a far greater degree than they do in ordinary humany blood. There is absolutely no clotting factor; yet, when their skin is broken the external tissue rejuvenates itself within seconds, thereby preventing excessive bleeding. This lack of clotting makes it impossible for thrombosis to occur and the overall arterial system is so supple and smooth within that they apparently never develop arteriosclerosis or artherosclerosis.

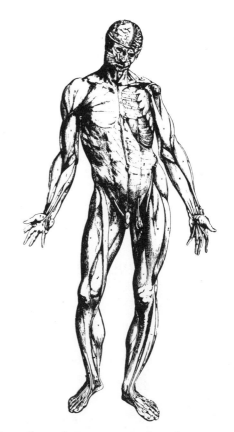

Vampires do not perspire, but secrete a slightly acidic oily substance which emits an

In the 1975 Fox-Rank film, Vampyres, *the two vampires, Fran and Miriam, are racing to beat the dawn in order to find a safe place of dark repose during the daylight hours.*

extremely offensive odor not unlike that of decaying flesh. This secretion appears to be bound up with their emotions, for when they are agitated, angry, frightened, or physically aroused the secretion increases by as much as 100 percent.

It is not surprising that they are essentially noctural in their habits, for to a greater or lesser degree they are photosensitive. Contrary to superstition they do not disintegrate in sunlight. It is the cause of great discomfort to them, however. Direct sunlight produces painful burning sensations which accelerate the metabolic activity rapidly. The result of this is that whatever blood they have stored in the stomach drains into the small intestine and is absorbed, leaving them in a state of acute discomfort on two levels. There is severe pain caused by the burning sensation of the sun, and sharp abdominal pain caused by hunger. The physical agony coupled with various chemical actions taking place in the body can cause a vampire to go berserk, at which time he or she becomes extremely dangerous. For this reason they shun direct sunlight, and when forced by circumstances to venture out during the brightest times of the day, they invariably wear highly protective clothing and dark eyeglasses. This extreme ocular photosensitivity causes their eyes to become bloodshot and subject to severe pain when exposed to the direct light of the sun. Also, in extreme instances there occurs profuse bleeding from the eyesockets. It is understandable, then, that in the days before tinted eyeglasses were available, vampires had no choice but to shun any activities during the daylight hours.

Their low body temperature and slow metabolic rate invites a comparison of sorts to cold-blooded creatures. Unlike reptiles, however, they, for obvious reasons avoid heat. When they sleep, they find the most comfort in cool or cold dark places. Their metabolism slows down, depending upon the temperature, to such a degree that they often assume a deathlike appearance. Observation of a sleeping vampire can be deceptive under conditions of substantial low temperature, for the respiration rate drops radically and it is difficult to detect any signs of life at all beyond a suppleness of the skin and, depending upon how recently the individual took nourishment, a certain ruddiness of complexion. In general, however, the complexion of the vampire is pale. The overall body structure is slender, well-proportioned, and totally lacking in fatty tissue.

A special research and education facility has been established on the island of Novaja Zemla near Russkaja Gavan, which is especially well suited for such a program. The isolation is ideal for security purposes and the cold climate is similarly appropriate. An ample supply of human blood is available, provided by volunteers who are housed in barracks in the facility.

Two years ago, following delivery of a report by the scientists who had worked on the project since its inception, a decision was made at the top governmental level. Approaches have been made to fellow socialist governments at the highest diplomatic echelon to launch an intensive recruitment program in Poland, Hungary, Romania, Czechoslovakia and the Democratic Republic of Germany. Response has been so successful that a dynamic Five-Year Plan is now well underway. It is a program which will take heretofore dangerous outcasts of society and transform them into useful productive members of the socialist world. We will now have thirty minutes of questions and answers.

In the 1969 A&E, Paragon quickie,
Blood of Dracula's Castle, *John
Carradine plays a vampire's assistant
who uses very modern methods of drawing blood for his master.*

Summary of Q & A Session

When an ordinary person becomes infected with the vampire syndrome it takes approximately one year before he or she becomes fully functional. Experiments have been made to determine whether or not vampires can alter their diet. Some success has been achieved with various high-protein liquid formulae, but results have not been 100 percent satisfactory. They cannot digest solid food. Some have developed a taste for fruit and vegetable juices, but only in a confectionary sense. These juices provide them with absolutely no nutrition. Alcohol, narcotics, and other drugs affect them much in the same way as normal persons are affected. Their sence of smell is very acute, but their own peculiar odor is not offensive to them. The old folk tales regarding their aversion to garlic are based on fact. Garlic, onions, leeks, and certain aromatic vegetables and herbs affect them with dizziness and nausea. They do not drink the blood of their own kind. They are instantly recognizable to one another by their distinctive smell. Experiments are underway to find an immune agent which will prevent them from infecting ordinary persons. In the research and education facility they do not make direct physical contact with their donors. Blood is extracted by means of standard medical procedures. They are capable of impregnating or being impregnated by normal members of the opposite sex. The offspring may or may not be born vampires. It is dependent upon dominant genes. In general their sex drives are lower than those of nonvampires. When they become personally involved with normals they employ colognes and deodorant preparations. They are most emphatically not animated corpses or "undeads" as the old superstition would have had people believe. The origin of the belief, however, is founded on a logical misunderstanding. In those instances where a vampire took blood from a single victim over an extended period of time, the victim developed very observable symptoms: lethargy, anemia, and eventually a deathlike coma, which invariably led to burial. Those interred in above-the-ground crypts invariably found a way to escape entombment. We have been told of rare instances where exceptionally hardy specimens, having been buried, succeeded in breaking their coffin lids and digging their way out. We have no concrete evidence to support this allegation, however. In conclusion and in answer to this last question, yes, the Soviet government has definite plans for these vampires when they have completed all of their reeducation and indoctrination. There are a sizeable number of areas where their unique qualities will enable them to perform duties of immense value to the state. I am at liberty to mention only one of these areas, and that is the guarding of prisoners, especially in large, remote locations. The implications are obvious. As for the other possibilities, I can only assure you, my dear comrades, that you will be informed well in advance of the public at large.

*A self-assured James Mason being
menaced by a vampire of the* Nosferatu
genre.

In the original 1931 version of Dracula, Bela Lugosi played the undead count without benefit of fangs. Orthodonture was not regarded as necessary until later versions.

Chapter 6

THE PERSONALITY OF THE VAMPIRE

As any vampirologist familiar with contemporary vampires will confirm, they have received an exceedingly "bad press" over the centuries. Looked upon as governed by demonic, satanic, and other evil influences, there was never any room for the slightest possibility that they were anything but totally malignant. These beliefs were reinforced periodically by the appearance of human monsters such as Elisabeth Bathory and others of her ilk.

Conversations with true vampires existing in the twentieth century have provided us with considerable insight, and consequently offer a far more realistic picture of their actual position. For obvious reasons they have always been forced to keep a low profile. Thus over the years they have, as a group, developed into rather quiet, low-key individuals. The last thing they wish to do is attract attention to themselves because, as they know all too well, more than anyone else possibly could, they constitute the ultimate minority group. And for purposes of better understanding, it would be advisable to regard them in this light.

Although in recent years a number of them throughout the world have managed with some success to establish an effective symbiotic relationship with sympathetic people, it is a relationship that is difficult to launch at the outset. Preconceptions, superstitions, fears, and suspicions play a major role in the task that the present-day vampire faces in coming out of the closet. As one vampire told an investigator to whom she had formed an attraction and admitted her true nature, "When people find out that you have to drink blood they think you're disgusting. Then after they think about it for a while they're frightened. So you just can't be too careful."

Perhaps one of the vampires' greatest advantages, given their difficult situation, is that they do seem to be immune to most human disease organisms. They tend to prefer living in large cities, where anonymity is easier to maintain, and where the opportunities to obtain blood are much greater than in rural areas.

Although it has been extremely difficult to conduct any sort of a definitive survey, a group of vampirologists from New York, Boston, Atlanta, Los Angeles, London, Barcelona, Paris, and Rio de Janeiro began keeping notes in the early 1960s and exchanging information on an annual basis. The results they obtained were significant and fascinating.

Although they have rarely admitted the fact to outsiders, vampires around the world make a serious effort to maintain loose ties. Their great fear is that, if the public at large were to become aware of them, the knowledge might engender conspiracy fears and prompt large-scale witch-hunts or widespread movements similar to the virulent anti-semitism that occurred in Germany during the Hitler era.

With very few exceptions vampires are scrupulously law-abiding. In general they pursue occupations that will keep them as far as possible from the public eye. Because of their physical photosensitivity they lean toward night work. They make exceptionally good night watchmen, first, because of their physical strength, and second, because of their ability to see in the dark. It is an almost unwritten rule in their ranks to select as victims individuals from the seamier side of society, those who, if fatally injured, will not be missed. They make every effort not to kill anyone, and always take meticulous precautions to avoid any excesses that would result in an increase in their population.

There are exceptions. At about the time of the publication of the book *Looking for Mr. Goodbar,* a young woman encountered a vampire from Hoboken, New Jersey, in a singles bar in the so-called "girl ghetto" of New York's upper East Side. Although an extremely attractive person, she had just turned thirty, and was depressed over the prospect of one day losing her physical attractiveness. As a result she embarked on a frantic odyssey of one-night stands, none of which were truly satisfying, but which, in some small measure, helped her to reinforce the conviction that she was still attractive to men.

During the course of her initial conversation with the vampire she expressed a fascination with the subject of vampirism, having recently seen an old Bela Lugosi film on late-night television. "How neat it would be if we could really become vampires," she said at one point in the evening. She went on to fantasize about how wonderful it would be for her to never need worry about losing her looks, to have power over others, to have a store of esoteric, inside knowledge denied to virtually everyone else whom she might meet.

She was slightly tipsy at the time, and the vampire, having had two bloody marys in order not to raise suspicions by abstaining entirely, was mildly affected by the alcohol himself. He accepted the young woman's invitation to come to her apartment and there he did a dangerous thing: he admitted to her that he was a vampire. At first she laughed at him, but having had a considerable amount to drink, she invited him to take some of her blood, saying, "Hey, that sounds like a crazy new kink. I like it." Not wishing to frighten her, he proposed making love first, and when she was naked in the throes of passion, he made a small incision in her neck with his fingernail and drank approximately one-half pint of her blood. She found the experience more intensely erotic than anything she had ever undergone before in her life. They repeated their lovemaking the next night, with even greater enthusiasm, and he stayed with her to make certain that no harm came to her. Thus began a strange love affair that resulted in her eventually becoming a full-fledged vampire. This particular incident, according to other vampires who have heard of it, is not an uncommon sort of occurrence.

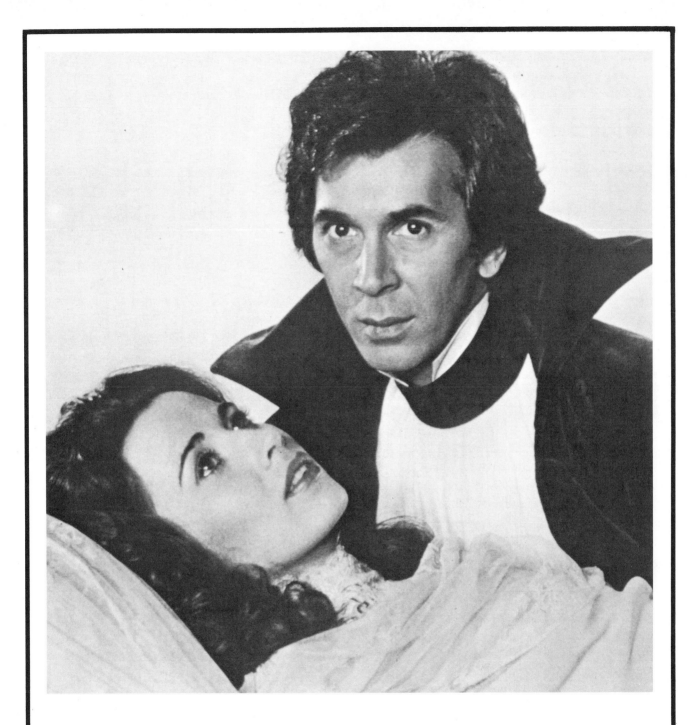

Although the underlying erotic element in Dracula *was played down a bit in Bram Stoker's novel and in the original film version, it was given full play in the 1979 release starring Frank Langella.*

It has been reported that a number of vampires find employment in blood banks logical, although they tend to prefer the commercial varieties rather than those affiliated with hospitals. The reason for this is that the commercial blood banks are frequented by a high percentage of derelicts and others from the fringes of society who make ideal victims.

Another favorite place of employment for them is funeral homes and hospital morgues. Accident victims and other newly deceased patients make a convenient and safe source of blood, for there is never any danger of their becoming vampires themselves. Furthermore, vampire morgue attendants, especially those working night shifts, have an ample opportunity to obtain the necessary nourishment with a minimum of difficulty.

A less widespread yet fairly popular occupation for vampires is that of attendant in mental hospitals. There they are relatively free to be quite open about themselves in the presence of patients. There has never been a single instance of a hospital staff member taking seriously the complaint from a patient that he or she has been attacked by a vampire.

There have been vampires who are known to have taken jobs as prison guards. The situation is not terribly dissimilar to that of a mental hospital, although there is a built-in danger factor. It is not pleasant to contemplate what could happen if, over the course of time, there evolved a class of criminal vampires. Socially responsible vampires are more aware of this than anyone and those who are employed in the prisons make every effort to protect society by taking every necessary precaution to prevent such a thing from happening. Frequently they take it upon themselves to deliberately cause the death of certain hardened criminals on the eve of their release from prison. It is their way of performing a valuable service for society that society cannot perform for itself.

There are not a great deal of data available about those vampires in our midst who function as the self-appointed eliminators of the more dangerous antisocial elements. This segment of vampire society, more than any other, must exercise extreme caution in the pursuit of its activities. From what little we have been able to glean about the areas in which they function, it is relatively reassuring to know that they are extremely responsible. In addition to those who work in the prisons, there are others who function on a regular basis in hospitals, particularly in those sections specializing in the care of the terminally ill. In most cases the hospital vampires serve as mercy killers, gently taking enough blood from the patients over a reasonable period of time, thereby hastening death. This is done most often in cases of those who are suffering great pain. And in so assisting these unfortunates, the vampires themselves undergo a certain degree of risk, for the drugs which are heavily concentrated in the patients' bloodstreams affect the vampires, causing them to experience considerable personal discomfort.

In many cases they have succeeded in bringing about what to the medical profession have appeared to be miraculous cures. Typical of this is the case of a young man who was dying of terminal lung cancer in a hospital in London. A female vampire, in the guise of a nurse, formed a strong attachment to the patient. Although serious deterioration had not yet set in, the carcinoma was metastatic and had spread to the liver, the stomach, the intestines, the pancreas, and the brain. It was only a matter of a month or so before the young man would die. The vampire began by taking small quantities of blood every day, making certain that the patient would have every opportunity to be infected with the

In the 1936 Universal film, Dracula's Daughter, *Otto Kruger takes Gloria Holden firmly in hand.*

The ABC-TV soap opera, Dark Shadows, *was the first television series to feature a vampire hero, Barnabas* Collins, *as portrayed by actor Jonathan Frid.*

vampire viroid. Within four weeks the organism spread throughout his system. His body began producing the vampiric antibodies which in turn attacked the cancer cells. Within six weeks there was not a trace of cancer. The patient was discharged, and with the assistance of the female vampire who saved him, moved to another community, where he is now a fully functional vampire performing work similar in nature to that of the female vampire who effectuated his recovery.

From what we have been able to ascertain about the general living habits of vampires today, it is very plain to see that they are very much a part of the world community. Though on the surface they appear to be part of all social classes, in reality they comprise a class of their own. In most instances they are concerned about being good citizens, but because of their distinct differences they must of necessity remain largely apart from the mainstream. They are apolitical. They are fearful of misunderstanding to a point of near-paranoia, for they are all too aware of how their forebears were persecuted, tortured, misunderstood, and hunted down like wild beasts. They have lived through and witnessed pogroms, witch hunts, and periods of mass hysteria in which countless innocent victims have been needlessly degraded and slaughtered. Yet through all of these upheavals they have always attempted to live useful lives and to survive, as have all persecuted minorities throughout history. Experience has taught them to be shy, circumspect, and cautious. As a result the average vampire is invariably courteous almost to a fault and introspective to the utmost degree. Except when their lives are threatened, vampires invariably back down from unpleasant confrontations. They make every effort to blend into the crowd and avoid all situations in which they are in danger of becoming conspicuous. They know that there is very little chance of their ever gaining true acceptance. You will never find them joining political movements or large social organizations, signing petitions, or becoming involved in any situation which might unexpectedly thrust them into the limelight. This is unfortunate in many ways, both for the vampires and the public at large. Many of them have abilities and talents that would enable them to be quite successful in pursuits which would focus attention on them.

During the era of the flower children a number of vampires experienced serious, unexpected difficulties directly related to the social upheavals of the 1960s. Many, in all innocence, chose young runaways as victims assuming, like so many others in straight society, that these youths were lost and beyond hope. Several groups of vampires made the error of forming hippie communes, expecting that there would exist a symbiosis between themselves and the young people whom they both supported and employed as suppliers of blood.

On the surface it appeared to be a good idea. The flower children were transient and there was little danger of any becoming vampires themselves. There was a constant flow of new faces. Unfortunately, many of them were from families prominent in their own communities and it soon became evident that they were being tracked down by police and private investigators. An equally serious problem that arose was the matter of drugs. Although the constitution of the vampire saved all of them from ever becoming addicted, many became seriously ill from the ingestion of blood heavily laden with narcotics, LSD, amphetamines, and other psychotropic substances.

Certainly one of the closest brushes with total disaster occurred in southern California when several vampires became involved with the notorious Manson family before it at-

In Andy Warhol's Blood for Dracula, *the unhappy count, played by Udo Keir, can only drink the blood of virgins.*

Here, he is sick to his stomach, having just drunk the wrong "vintage."

tained its international infamy. The vampires, three women and a man, remained with the Manson group for several months in the beginning, but were soon forced to leave because they would not come under the hypnotic influence of Charles Manson. Their instincts told them that the man and his followers were potentially dangerous and they deemed it inadvisable to permit the family members to become vampires themselves. They also recognized that there would eventually arise a potentially dangerous confrontation that could only lead to exposure, so the vampires wisely left the group. "Had we only anticipated the tragic consequences of the Manson family's potential for evil," said one of them, "we would have made certain that none of them would have survived contact with us."

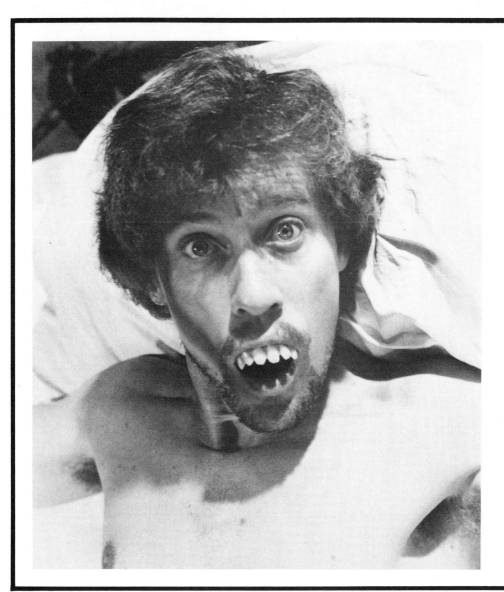

The most striking aspect of the vampire's personality is his or her physical attractiveness to the opposite sex. There is also a similarly powerful attraction for the same sex that is governed by hunger. This magnetic quality possessed by all vampires is nature's gift, ensuring the perpetuation of the species. Although the sex drive of the vampire is substantially lower than that of the ordinary human, all vampires are reported to be exceptional lovers, far superior to their selected victims or partners. There is a solid reason for this. First, they are far more experienced than their fully human counterparts, and second, they have complete control over their own bodies. Whereas the average human female is infinitely more capable sexually than the male, the male vampire has an endurance factor equal to that of his female counterpart. Furthermore, all vampires are gentle, despite their immense strength. If it were not for the combined qualities of their psychological and physical natures, it would have been impossible for them to have survived as long as they did, and to have coexisted with such success.

*Christopher Lee as Dracula is impaled in
the Hammer/Warner production,*
Dracula A.D. 1972.

Chapter 7

DEALING WITH VAMPIRES

In view of current knowledge about vampires, the traditional methods of "dealing" with them are suddenly thrust into a new light: they are cruel, inhumane, and needless. Consequently, when we examine them here we must do so from a viewpoint which will enable us to better understand the plight of the vampire today. To reemphasize a point which has been made earlier, the vampire was always regarded by society as an outsider—feared, loathed, hunted down, and destroyed. Many of the traditional methods of the past employed to put vampires to death were simply atrocious means of destroying them. These evolved as a result of an accumulation of erroneous knowledge about vampires, and empirical knowledge that they were not easily killed by more traditional means.

It must always be borne in mind that vampires were never given the benefit of the doubt, but were universally looked upon as enemies of mankind. Because of this prevalent belief structure, many practices that gained wide acceptance as necessary prerequisites to the destruction of a vampire were in reality purely ritual in nature. A number of these had their roots in superstition and religious beliefs. Still others had no bearing on the actual killing of vampires, but merely served as so-called protections against them.

Superstitious East European peasants often hung whitethorn and buckthorn on the windows and doors of their houses to ward off the intrusion of vampires. This practice stemmed from a tradition dating back to ancient Greece, when it was customary to fasten thorny branches around windows and doors in order to prevent evil spirits or witches from entering. There is a relationship between whitethorn and Christianity itself. According to tradition, Jesus' crown of thorn was fashioned from this shrub. In the Slavic countries, the use of thorns was more pragmatic and more closely related to the ancient Greek practice. It was believed that vampires would become entangled in the thorns, and that this would confuse them.

Another strange belief was that if millet seeds were sprinkled about the grave of a suspected vampire, the vampire, for some mysterious reason, would be forced to bend over and pick them all up before being able to go forth in search of victims.

There were other precautionary measures taken by superstitious peasants designed to protect them from vampires. Most were relatively harmless procedures which in actuality had no effect whatever upon vampires. For example, in Romania certain old women in small villages were thought to possess special talents enabling them to successfully deal with vampires. Sometimes they would drive nails through the heads of corpses suspected of being vampires. If the body did in fact happen to be that of a true vampire, one that had been interred in a crypt above ground, such an action might easily prove fatal. Another custom involved the slaughtering of a pig on the feast of St. Ignatius, five days before Christmas. The body of the suspected corpse was then rubbed with the fat rendered from the pig. Other precautions taken in Eastern Europe included opening the grave of a suspected vampire, filling it with straw, impaling the body with a stake of hawthorn, then igniting the straw and maintaining the blaze until the body was completely cremated. In view of the fact that this method was usually restricted to bodies which had been buried for some time, there was little chance of its being used against a true vampire.

The practice of driving stakes through the bodies of suspected vampires was universal, and has been so widely publicized in fiction and motion pictures that little more need be said about it. A more modern refinement of this, popular in Romania after the advent of firearms, was to fire a bullet through the coffin. It was believed that the bullet would be rendered more effective it were made of silver and blessed by a priest before its use. Another precaution taken in some areas of Romania was simply to walk around a suspected vampire's grave exhaling smoke from a cigar, cigarette, or pipe on the anniversary of the suspect's death. Still another of the less fearful methods was to stuff the mouth of the corpse with garlic, or to place the thorny branch of a wild rose on the grave.

Some of the more grisly methods of dealing with suspected vampires were to decapitate the corpses, cut out the hearts and burn them, then to sprinkle the ashes on the grave. In Bulgaria and Serbia whitethorn was often placed in the navel of the corpse. All hair was shaved from the body except for the head, the soles of the feet were slit, and finally a nail was driven in the back of the head.

Brief mention should be made here about the superstitious belief that vampires cannot stand the sight of crucifixes, icons, and other holy symbols of Christianity. This of course is sheer nonsense. As a matter of fact many vampires deliberately wear crucifixes for the express purpose of preventing others from suspecting their true nature.

Fortunately the old barbaric depredations against corpses and vampires do not occur today, with the possible exception of instances among remote primitive peoples and members of satanic cults who practice bizarre rituals unrelated to vampirism. What is important for us to know today is how we should deal with vampires in the event that we chance to encounter them. To begin with, it is essential to bear in mind at all times that there is nothing to fear from the majority of them. Most will never attempt to take blood from any individual who is not willing to supply it. Bearing this in mind, it is essential to know that if one does indeed meet a vampire and is willing to supply him or her with blood, the matter must first be discussed thoroughly and openly. Next, a method of extraction must be mutually agreed upon that is safe, painless, and hygienic. It is important to let the vampire know whether or not you are on any medication which might

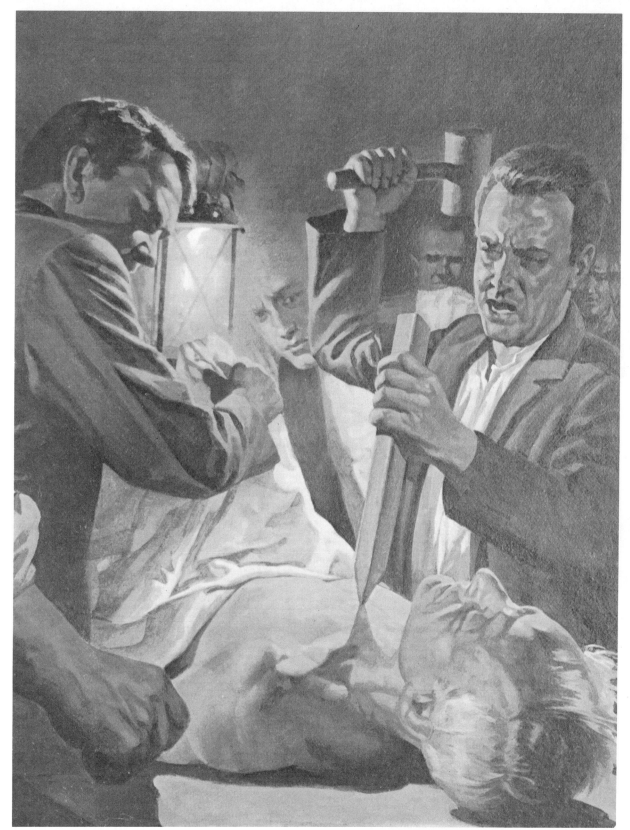

The destruction of a vampire by the traditional method of hammering a stake through his heart.

Jack Palance as a very credible Dracula, meeting his end via a wooden stake.

affect the structure of your blood or be carried in the bloodstream. There are certain drugs which, though not dangerous to vampires, may cause them physical discomfort. Such medications will invariably preclude the user's becoming a donor. Since very few individuals today have any great interest in becoming vampires themselves, there is no necessity for physical contact if it is not mutually wanted. Of course, there are instances where the erotic element is present, at which time physical contact may be desired. The viroid organism which ultimately leads to vampirism is slow-acting and a few physical contacts properly spaced in time are perfectly harmless. Many vampires today employ standard medical transfusion equipment and, because of their great experience in drawing blood, are in the majority of cases far more skilled in the extraction process than many medical personnel in blood banks and hospitals. How many patients have suffered needless pain, discomfort, and epidermal discoloration caused by inexperienced

Christopher Neame and Caroline Munro in Dracula A.D. 1972.

technicians, interns, and nurses taking blood samples for tests?

Because the vampire when drinking blood experiences a sense of exhilaration akin to that of sexual satisfaction in the ordinary human, it is conceivable that one might occasionally get carried away while ingesting blood through physical contact. All vampires are fully aware of this, and consequently they tend as a rule to prefer extracting the blood first and drinking it afterward, as a safety measure for the donor.

A word of caution should be given concerning those rare instances when one encounters the occasional irresponsible vampire who attempts to take blood from an unwilling victim. It is advisable in such cases to avoid struggling. The vampire's superior strength precludes successful resistance. Under the circumstances an immediate admission of a willingness to cooperate will save the victim from receiving any unnecessary physical injury which might ensue from a struggle. It is sometimes possible to dissuade the vampire and convince him or

Dramatic juxtaposition of symbolism—good and evil—in the 1971 Hammer production, Twins of Evil, *which based its characters loosely on* Sheridan Le Fanu's Carmilla *and placed them against a background of fanatical witch hunters in Cromwellian England.*

her that it would be advisable to seek another victim. If this is not feasible, then immediately discuss the matter thoroughly and decide on a method of withdrawal which will be most convenient and likely to cause the least discomfort. It should be emphasized here, however, that the eventuality of such an attack occurring is extremely unlikely. The odds against it are approximately 3,200 to 1.

Essentially, then, dealing with a vampire today is for the most part no different from dealing with anyone who in some way or another is not like you. For example, vegetarians and nonvegetarians are quite able to take meals together if each respects and understands the other and neither attempts to proselytize or force the other to change eating habits. Heterosexuals and homosexuals are quite capable of enjoying nonsexual friendships. Men and women can be friends or associates without the sexual element. Individuals with diametrically opposing political views may enjoy a personal relationship that is devoid of political content. There have been instances on the international intelligence scene where spies employed by nominally opposing governments have formed strong bonds of friendship based upon their mutual professionalism, understanding, and respect, not to mention strong common interests. With whom else can they talk shop?

For this reason it is quite possible for vampires and nonvampires to establish and maintain strong bonds of friendship. Vampires are loyal friends and lovers. They are deeply appreciative of understanding and respect. Because of their dietary restrictions they must be takers, thus they more than compensate by giving in other areas.

Not long ago a group of vampires living in southern California succeeded in establishing friendly ties with a substantial group of neighbors in their community. The nonvampires with whom this relationship was established were not only thoroughly understanding, they proved over a period of time to be completely trustworthy. No one outside the community other than certain vampires living elsewhere has, to this day, any knowledge of the actual state of affairs. They even went so far as to establish a night softball series. The enterprise was entered into by everyone with great enthusiasm. Unfortunately it failed, but with a goodnatured conclusion. It developed that the vampires, because of their superior strength and endurance, proved unbeatable. The nonvampires were absolutely no match for them. As a result they disbanded the league and a film society-discussion group was formed instead.

This is an encouraging sign, a sign that old fears and barriers can be broken down, that there is hope for better mutual understanding between vampire and nonvampire in the future to the benefit of all.

THE FRENCH NOBLEMAN
WHO WAS A VAMPIRE

In Another Grey Ghost Book, *by Jessie Adelaide Middleton, the following account of a lesser-known French vampire appears.*

A French viscount—de Morième by name—was one of the few French noblemen who managed to retain their estates during the troublous times of the French Revolution. He was an extraordinary looking man, very tall and thin, with a high, almost pointed forehead, and protruding teeth. Under an air of suave courtesied kindness he concealed a ferociously cruel disposition, which showed itself when the fires of the great revolution had burned themselves out, and all was once more quiet. To get level as it were, with the working classes, he sent for his retainers and workpeople one by one, and, after he had interviewed them, cut off their heads. It is not surprising to hear that, in return, he himself met his death by assassination at the hands of some of the peasantry.

No sooner, however, was the viscount laid in the grave than an appalling number of young children died in the neighborhood, all of whom bore vampire marks on their throats. Later on, when he had been buried for some time, and while the tomb was being repaired, there were nine more cases in a single week. The awful slaughter went on till seventy-two years passed away, and the viscount's grandson succeeded to the title.

Young de Morième, hearing the appalling stories of his grandfather, consulted a priest with the idea of laying to rest his horrible ancestor's ghost, and, after some discussion and delay, it was decided to open the tomb. The services of a man specially successful in such cases were obtained; the vault was opened in the presence of the authorities.

Every coffin was found to have undergone the usual process of rotting away, except that of the old viscount, which after seventy-two years, was perfectly strong and sound. The lid was removed and the body found quite fresh and free from decomposition. The face was flushed and there was blood in the heart and chest. The skin was soft and natural. New nails had grown on the hands and feet.

The body was removed from the coffin and a whitethorn driven by the expert through the heart of the corpse, with the ghastly result that the blood and water poured forth and the corpse groaned and screamed. Then the remains were burned on the seashore; and from that day the child deaths ceased and there were no more serious crimes in the neighborhood.

From *Another Grey Ghost Book,*
by Jessie Adelaide Middleton

Lon Chaney, Sr., in the silent film, London After Midnight, *in which he plays a detective who dons a vampire disguise for the purpose of catching a criminal.*

Released originally in the U.S. as Blood of Dracula *in 1957 by American International, this film capitalized on the '50s* *phenomenon of* I Was a Teenage Frankenstein, I Was a Teenage Werewolf, *etc.*

Chapter 8

WEREWOLVES, FOX LADIES, AND OTHER CHILDREN OF THE NIGHT

There is a general tendency among those not thoroughly familiar with the subject to mention werewolves in the same breath as vampires. For that reason it would be appropriate to digress here briefly and devote some attention to the subject of lycanthropy. The word lycanthropy is derived from the Greek words *lykos* = wolf and *anthropos* = man. Psychiatry defines the word as a delusion in which men believe themselves capable of transforming themselves into wolves. In general, however, the word is used more broadly, referring to the overall phenomenon of humans undergoing metamorphosis into animals. Although there has never been any hard evidence to support the belief that humans were ever able to actually transform themselves into wolves or any other beasts, the superstition has existed in virtually every culture on the face of the earth. In Western culture the best-known lycanthropic belief pertains to humans becoming wolves. In non-Western cultures, however, legends and tales exist in which humans become tigers, foxes, leopards, jaguars, lions, hyenas, elephants, and even crocodiles.

It is interesting to note that in many parts of Europe it was once believed that when a werewolf died it became a vampire, which to a degree helps to explain a tendency to connect the two today. The principal reason, however, for an association in the mind between vampires and werewolves has always been that both were objects of terror. Whereas superstitious peasants believed that vampires were animated corpses, werewolves, on the other hand, were regarded as very much alive. Though there were never any instances in which individuals voluntarily became vampires, there are any number of authenticated accounts on record of mentally deranged persons swearing under oath that by making pacts with the devil, or by performing sorcery, they could metamorphose into wolves and wreak vengeance upon their enemies. During the height of the witch mania in the sixteenth and seventeenth centuries, there were also werewolf trials.

One of the most celebrated took place in Bordeaux, France, in the early seventeenth century. The werewolf's name was Jean Grenier and at his trial he claimed to have killed and eaten over fifty young girls and women during his periods as a wolf. It is interesting to observe that though many of the witches tried during this period were convicted and burned at the stake, Grenier was adjudged insane and committed to a mental institution for the rest of his life where, it was reported later, he became a good Christian toward the end.

One did not become a werewolf only by making a pact with the Evil One, or by working magic. According to popular belief a person could become afflicted with lycanthropy accidentally by eating certain plants said to have a lycanthropous property, by drinking water from lycanthropous brooks, or from indentations left by wolves' footprints that had collected water. In some regions lycanthropy was said to be hereditary.

The black magic involved in acquiring the ability to become a werewolf was difficult

Sixteenth-century woodcut depicting a werewolf attacking its victim.

and complicated. The ritual had to be performed in a remote area, far from any populated place. Solitary forests and mountain tops were considered to be especially propitious. Not only was the proper place of vital importance, so was the time. The most favorable time was a night of a new moon on the cusp of the seventh house cojoined with Saturn in opposition to Jupiter.

At midnight, on a level piece of ground, the candidate had to mark a circle not less than fourteen feet in diameter. In the center of the circle another circle, six feet in diameter, had to be inscribed. At the center of the inner circle it was necessary to erect an iron tripod holding an iron pot of water, under which a fire had to be built. As soon as the water began to boil, handfuls of any three

Woodcut attributed to 15th-century artist Lucas Cranach of a wild man, or werewolf, carrying off a human victim.

of the following substances had to be thrown into the pot:

- Asafetida
- Aloe
- Hemlock
- Henbane
- Nightshade (any variety of the genus *solanum*)
- Opium
- Parsley
- Poppy seed
- Saffron

Next, the following incantation had to be made:

Spirits from the deep
Who never sleep,
Be kind to me.

Spirits from the grave
Without a soul to save,
Be kind to me.

Spirits of the trees
That grow upon the leas,
Be kind to me.

Spirits of the air,
Foul and black, not fair,
Be kind to me.

Water spirits hateful,
To ships and bathers fateful,
Be kind to me.

Spirits of earthbound dead
That glide with noiseless tread,
Be kind to me.

Spirits of heat and fire,
Destructive in your ire,
Be kind to me.

Spirits of cold and ice,
Patrons of crime and vice,
Be kind to me.

Wolves, vampires, satyrs, ghosts!
Elect of all the devilish hosts!
I pray you send hither,
Send hither, send hither,
The great gray shape that makes men shiver!
Come! Come! Come!

Sixteenth-century conception of anthropomorphic were-creatures.

Next the candidate had to strip to the waist and smear his body with the fat of a freshly killed animal, preferably a cat, mixed with a blend of anise seed, camphor, and opium. When this was done, the next step was to bind the loins with a wolf skin, kneel down within the inner circle, and wait for the spirit that had been summoned to appear. It was believed that when the fire burned with a blue flame and died out the manifestation was about to occur. Sometimes it was said to appear after a terrifying clamor of shrieks, groans, crashes, and thunderous sounds. Sometimes it remained invisible, and made itself felt by a sensation of acute cold and feelings of terror. Other manifestations were said to be in the form of a hunter, a monster, half-human, half-beast, and still others as an amorphous, partially materialized form which was poorly defined.

It is easy to understand how individuals employing such ingredients under such fear-inspiring circumstances could easily induce self-hypnosis, which would enable them to believe that they had undergone a true supernatural experience.

There were other ways to become a werewolf as well. Sometimes it was merely the result of having been cursed. Occasionally it was a punishment for some terrible misdeed, and in other instances it was a matter of sheer bad luck. There is an old Irish legend which tells that St. Patrick occasionally punished people by causing them to be transformed into wolves. In one of these he is said to have inflicted this penalty on a Welsh king, and in another he supposedly cursed an entire clan so that not only they but their descendants were doomed to become werewolves at a certain time every seventh year.

The folklore of the werewolf, like that of the vampire, is both diverse and fascinating. It also has a venerable tradition. Indeed, one of the earliest recorded narratives containing an anecdote about lycanthropy is the *Satyricon* of Petronius. It is only a minor incident in the novel, and deals with someone who fought off an attack by a wolf on a road, wounding it in the leg. Later a wounded soldier is encountered in the home of a friend. The injury corresponded to that which was inflicted on the wolf, and it is revealed that the soldier was indeed a lycanthrope.

The range and scope of werewolf tales is considerably wider than that of those about vampires. Many of these tales revolve around werewolves who are hapless victims of the lycanthropic curse. They do not wish to be werewolves, they do not want to injure their fellow men, yet when the time of metamorphosis comes upon them they are driven by forces beyond their control and impelled to commit atrocious deeds. The unfortunate heroes of such stories, knowing all too well the implications of their dreadful fate, exert all their efforts to protect those whom they want to save from the savage attacks of the wolf lurking within them.

There is the tale of the man-wolf who knows that he is doomed to spend twenty-four hours as a wolf once every month. At one point he is stranded on a desert island with his beautiful mistress. On the eve of his metamorphosis, knowing that when it comes upon him he will lose all vestiges of humanity, he leaves her and puts great distance between them so that there will be no danger of his destroying her.

On the other side of the coin there are tales of benign werewolves. In an old French legend, a monk leaves his monastery one day to attend a country fair. He overindulges in food and drink and sets out to return in a slightly tipsy state. He is attacked by a pack of ferocious wolves when suddenly a larger, more powerful wolf appears on the scene and savagely attacks the wolfpack. In so doing the creature sustains a number of injuries, but it successfully drives off the other wolves and escorts the terrified monk back to his monastery. The resolution of the story is that the werewolf was actually the abbot himself, who afterward reprimands the monk for his excesses and imposes a stiff penance on him with a stern warning to mend his ways.

In some parts of Europe it was believed that werewolves were attracted to precious jewels, and there are tales concerning this predilection. In one, a vain young woman, the wife of a fat, stodgy man over twenty years her senior, yearned to attend a series of gala balls that happened to be given on a single night. Her husband was willing to go to one, but insisted on going home early. The wife, eager to show off her diamond tiara, necklace, and bracelets, drugged her husband's brandy, rearranged her hair and jewels, then slipped out of the house and danced until well after midnight.

Dozing in her carriage on the way home, she was suddenly awakened by a cough, and to her terror discovered that she was not

Les Lupins, *or The Wolves, by Maurice Sand. These werewolves are seen by the artist as retaining a semblance of their human form.*

alone. Seated opposite her was a handsome young man with large dark eyes and gleaming white teeth, impeccably attired in evening clothes. When he told her that he had been attracted to her jewels she feared the worst. He must be a jewel thief. Laughingly he assured her that stealing her diamonds was the furthest thing from his mind.

The stranger seemed to know a great deal about her, that she was unhappily married, and that she had drugged her husband that night. When he learned that the man was fat, he grew intensely interested. He declared that he and his servant, who was driving the carriage, were werewolves. He offered to spare the young woman's life if she would give him the keys to her house. Thinking him a madman bent on robbery, she complied with his request. He then had his servant tie her to a tree in a deserted section of the woods, and drove off in the coach.

Shortly afterward the man and his servant returned bearing between them the unconscious form of the drugged husband.

They untied the woman, urged her to flee for her life, and helped her into the driver's seat of the carriage. As she drove off she could hear the baleful howling of the wolves intermingled with the agonized shrieks of her unfortunate husband. But the only thought that crossed her mind was a deep sense of thankfulness that she still had all her jewels.

Another variant on the werewolf theme is that of the witch or sorcerer who uses black magic to become a wolf at will. Folklorists assert that the fairy tale "Hansel and Gretel" is a variation of this sort, as is "Little Red Riding Hood." A lesser-known tale in this vein appears in the literature of France. It concerns a pathetic young man who is the ugliest male in the village, and as such constantly subject to rejection and ridicule. On the outskirts of the village lives a beautiful witch. She lures him to her cottage with flattery and coquetry, serving him sumptuous meals day after day until he becomes quite fat, after which she turns into a wolf and devours him.

Eighteenth-century drawing of the so-called Wild Beast of Gévaudan, said to have killed and eaten over a hundred residents of a French village during 1764 and 1765.

One of the prevalent beliefs associated with werewolves was that they could only be killed with a silver dagger or bullet. In a story written by Jane Rice in the 1940s, a plump American female gourmande, living in Paris at the outbreak of World War II, becomes distressed at the prospect of meat rationing because it interferes with her feasts. One day she encounters a mysterious naked youth in her garden whom she takes into her house. She quickly discovers that he is a werewolf. At the point of his metamorphosis she pops a chocolate-covered silver bullet into his mouth, thereby causing him to choke to death, after which she turns the table and devours him.

Another dominant theme in lycanthropic folklore concerns the righteous revenge of helpless individuals upon their persecutors. In a story uncovered by the late Anglo-Irish occultist Elliot O'Donnell, a Dutch trader in South America encounters two young Arawak Indian children who live with a wretched old hag in a remote Amazon village. The young brother and sister are mercilessly mistreated by the old woman, who perpetually abuses them verbally and physically.

She complains to the Dutchman that all the two ever do is run off into the jungle and talk to evil spirits. One day the man bribes the old woman to stop mistreating the children, at which time the little girl says to him, "May the spirit of the jungle protect you." He questions her and her brother afterward, and they explain that the old woman is not their mother, that their real mother is the spirit of the jungle who would soon punish the old woman once and for all.

He is about to dismiss this when he observes the two scamper off into the jungle at dusk. On an impulse he follows them. Eventually they come to a clearing. Making every effort to conceal himself, he watches them closely. In the midst of the clearing is a shimmering pool that glitters with silvery streaks of moonlight. In the center of the pool he notices the most immense water lily he has ever seen. Its petals and stalk seem to glow with an eerie light of their own. Suddenly he is diverted by the sound of the two children, hand in hand, kneeling down before the pool, muttering an incantation in a tongue he has never heard.

An unexpected breeze begins to blow and the Dutchman is seized by a strange vertigo. His vision blurs and everything before his eyes appears unreal and out of phase. Paralyzed with fear he observes an amorphous blob rise silently from the depths of the pool. Where the children had been standing are now two glowing spheres of a greenish irridescent hue that sway and expand before his eyes. As suddenly as the phenomenon occurred everything returns to normal, and in place of the children there are now two sleek jaguars with luminescent yellow eyes. Seizing his rifle he prepares to be attacked, but the two jungle cats merely contemplate him calmly and make no move to spring. Instead, turning around, they bound off into the jungle.

After hours of torturous effort to retrace his steps through the tangled vegetation, he finally returns to the village from which he had come. Exhausted and ravenous, he comes to the house of the old woman and the two children. As he approaches it he hears peculiar crunching noises from within. They remind him of the cracking and grinding of splintering wood—or bone. Pausing before the door, he listens for a moment, then knocks, at which the sounds cease. Summoning up his courage he pushes the door open and peers into the dim interior. At first he sees nothing, but then as his eyes grow accustomed to the dark, they are assailed by a sight he knows he will never forget if he lives

The 1971 Hammer MGM/EMI film, Lust for a Vampire, *was one of the many spinoffs of Le Fanu's* Carmilla, *offering a variation of the vampire-lesbian theme.*

to be old as Methuselah. There in the corner of the room are the torn, half-eaten remains of the old woman, and crouching alongside are the two children, blood-smeared and wide-eyed, voraciously munching on what had once been a human arm.

Although there are stories of werewolves in China, they are less prevalent than tales of were-tigers; these also abound in India, Malaysia, Indonesia, and Indochina. Qualitatively most of the stories are similar to those of the European werewolf. Certainly the most fascinating were-creatures of the East are the fox ladies of China and Japan. There is a major difference between these and their wolf counterparts. Rather than being humans who metamorphose into animal shape, they are animals who transform themselves into humans. Traditionally, fox ladies are beautiful, seductive, often mischievous creatures. Often they form strong attachments to human males, falling in love, entering into long relationships, and frequently bearing their human lovers children who are half-fox.

In the literature of China ghosts often manifest themselves in the same fashion as foxes and display a similar set of behavior patterns. In a classic tale written by the immortal seventeenth-century author P'u Sung

Chinese concept of headless monsters alleged to have been seen by Crusaders in the Holy Land.

形天神圖

Ling, a fox and a ghost both fall in love with a poor young scholar. They come to him on alternate nights and convince him that they are human "singing girls," or village prostitutes. He soon becomes exhausted to the point of death. The fox lady comes finally and confronts the ghost, pointing out to her that if she truly loves the young scholar, she must stop her nocturnal amours because for a human to make love to a ghost over an extended period of time is ultimately fatal. The beautiful little ghost is remorseful and joins forces with the fox lady to nurse the young man back to health. Afterward the fox bears him a son, the ghost is reincarnated and returns as a human girl, and eventually the three of them go off together and live happily ever after.

In my book *Vampires, Werewolves and Ghouls*, I write:

Anthropologists tell us that lycanthropy is rooted in totemism, the belief by some primitive peoples in a blood relationship between themselves and certain favored animals. American Indians frequently took personal and tribal names from animals. The Makanga of Central Africa still believe that witches are capable of transforming themselves into leopards, crocodiles, and hyenas. Back in the 1930s members of the Anyoto tribe, belonging to the dread secret society of leopard men, went on a rampage of killings in what was then the Belgian Congo. Dressing in costumes of bark painted with yellow and black spots they stalked their enemies in the jungle, bursting into villages to drag them from their homes where they slaughtered them with claw-shaped knives which they held between clenched fists. Afterwards they had ritual cannibalistic feasts, and when they were finished they left whatever remained to be strewn around like the human leavings of wild animals. More recently, in 1946, still another gang of leopard men terrorized a village near Lagos, and a year later stories appeared in London newspapers about lion-men in Tanganyika who, before being captured, killed nearly fifty victims.

PORPHYRIA

Porphyria is the name given to a group of rare diseases which, in olden days, very likely prompted the belief that sufferers were vampires. Porphyria victims display a number of symptoms, including blotchy discoloration of the skin. Sometimes a reddening of the teeth occurs. Nails and skin may fluoresce. Patients may become irritable, restless, psychotic, confused, subject to anxiety, hallucination, and delirium. The urine can be red or pink and in certain cases the skin develops a condition of photosensitivity, causing those afflicted with the disease to shun sunlight.

In the late 1960s a story appeared in the *New York Times* about the conviction of a witch doctor in an emerging African nation. For a small fee he had agreed, on terms negotiated with a client, to transform himself into a crocodile, after which he would devour the man's mother-in-law. He explained that in his professional opinion this method was the best way of eliminating the woman. Unfortunately the two had a disagreement shortly afterward on the matter of the fee, despite the fact that the necessary sorcery had already been performed satisfactorily. The dispute soon grew to such proportions that news of the matter reached the authorities. As a result both the witch doctor and his client were arrested and tried. Both were convicted and sentenced to death. Both men immediately appealed. Although the convictions were upheld by the supreme court, it was decided that the crime which had been committed was not conspiracy and murder, but rather conspiracy to commit unlawful sorcery and illegal metamorphosis into a crocodile, which had led to the death of a citizen.

It has been suggested by psychologists that the belief in lycanthropy stems from wish-fantasies in minds of the poor, the oppressed, and the helpless, that creatures like the wolf and the tiger are logical animals to emulate and indeed to become by means of magic. They are hardy, swift, powerful, and bloodthirsty. In the case of the wolf, the sound of its howling alone was enough in less enlightened days to inspire terror in the hearts of those within range of its mournful voice. Furthermore, in bygone times wolves were always more dangerous during winter time and at night. Food was harder to obtain and hunger drove them to make desperate attacks. Was it natural, then, for men to identify wolves with darkness, cold, and death? Certainly even today anyone who has ever heard the distant howling of a wolf on a dark night can easily identify with the terror that this baneful cry must have instilled in its hearers in times when darkness was in men's hearts even when the warm rays of the sun lighted their path by day.

Sixteenth-century French version of an English werewolf.

BLOOD, MYTH, AND EMOTION

How often have we heard squeamish people cry out, "Oh, I can't stand the sight of blood!" How many times have we heard of strong, hearty men fainting dead away at the sight of blood gushing from a wound? The reasons for such reactions are buried deep within the human race, and predate recorded history by millenia. Primitive man, when he was scarcely above the level of the ape, recognized at once that there was a relationship between blood and life. When the body was slashed by savage beasts or hacked by the weapons of enemies, life ebbed as the precious red fluid drained from the unfortunate victim. Consequently, as man's mental capacity increased, and along with it his imagination, he attributed magical properties to blood. Recognizing that without blood life ceased to exist, he grew to fear any situation which involved its loss. Along this path of logic arose the rituals and taboos surrounding birth, loss of virginity, death, and even the menstrual flux of women. There is much to be said for the theory that the fear of women during their menstrual period contributed much toward their relegation to an inferior position by men.

Pliny wrote that all sorts of dreadful things would result from contact with menstrual blood. Wine would turn sour, fields would become unfruitful, knives would become blunted, and mirrors would lose their luster. He went on to assert that dogs who lapped menstrual blood would go mad, and their bites would be so poisonous that there was no known cure. In Lebanon it was believed that the shadow of a menstruating woman would cause flowers to wither, trees to rot, and snakes to die away. In spite of such beliefs, however, there were those

elsewhere who believed that menstrual blood was a vital ingredient for love potions.

In view of such attitudes it is thoroughly understandable that over the centuries misconceptions and superstitions would multiply, spread, and become complex. That beliefs connected with blood became deeply intermingled with sexual concepts was only natural, for blood, sex, life, and death were too closely linked to have ever been considered separately, whether consciously or unconsciously. Sexual intercourse with a virgin spilled blood, the birth of a child involved the loss of blood, and death by violence accompanied the shedding of blood. How natural, then, that when men dreamed of demons and monsters they should lust after blood, the very essence of life itself. How very understandable that some men would believe that the drinking of blood, especially the blood of brave fighters or powerful animals, would impart strength, bravery, or magical protection.

No discussion of the symbolism of blood can be complete without at least a passing reference to the sacrificial and other blood rites. Blood sacrifices are so much a part of the heritage of mankind that it would be impossible to cover, even in a single volume, a complete history of the subject. At some time in the development of all peoples there existed a dark period during which human sacrifices were made. A particularly gruesome blood rite of ancient times was the Taurobolium, described by Royden Keith Yerkes in his book, Sacrifice in Greek and Roman Religions and Early Judaism. *It apparently originated in the area of Persia and consisted of the following: a neophyte who* was undergoing an initiation ceremony was placed underneath a specially built wooden platform that had been punctured with holes. Above on the platform itself a bull was slain. As the fresh blood of the animal dripped down through the holes, the neophyte wallowed in it, rubbing it all over his body, his face, and his head. During the course of the ceremony appropriate ritualistic music was played and sung by the other celebrants. The purpose of the Taurobolium was to impart the strength and courage of the bull to the initiate, through the magical properties of the blood.

The belief in such magical properties of blood has led to its use in a multitude of ways by many different peoples as a means of protection against evil. Agricultural tribes smeared blood on trees to stop droughts. Hunting tribes dipped tips of their weapons in the blood of wild beasts after killing them, in order to protect themselves from the wrath of the animals' ghosts. Other tribes, who believed that adultery brought on certain disaster, would slaughter a pig and pour its blood into a furrow that had been dug in the ground. Even in the Jewish and Christian traditions blood has played a significant role. In Exodus the children of Israel are ordered by God to slay lambs before the last of the terrible Egyptian plagues. They are instructed to smear the blood on the door posts of their houses.

And the blood shall be to you for a token upon the houses where Ye are: and when I see the blood I shall pass over you, and the plague shall not be upon you to destroy you when I smite the land of Egypt. (Exod. 12:13).

During the consecration of the wine at Mass, the priest says, Hic est enim calix sanguinis mei (this is the chalice of my blood). At this time it is believed by the participants that Christ mystically dies again on the altar, and that the chalice of wine changes into his actual blood. Even this ceremony in its highly refined state is a sort of atavism which symbolically links the modern believer to his ancestor who drank actual blood so that it would protect him or endow him with the qualities of the victim who shed it.

The first evidence of any shrinking from the barbarism of drinking blood appears in the Old Testament in Leviticus 17:10: And whatsoever men there be of the House of Israel, or of the strangers who sojourn among you, that eateth any manner of blood; I will even set my face against that soul that eateth blood, and will cut him off from among his people.

This is further emphasized in Leviticus 17:14: For it is the life of all flesh, the blood of it is for the life thereof; therefore I said unto the children of Israel, Ye shall not eat the blood of no manner of flesh; for the life of all flesh is the blood thereof: whosoever eateth it shall be cut off.

Living under such stern admonitions, it is no wonder that the Jews and the early Christians rebelled so bitterly against the Romans and their bloody gladiatorial sports. Yet despite their teachings and beliefs, even these people could not always control the animal spark that lurked deep within their unconscious. St. Augustine in his Confessions tells the story of Alypius, a young friend of his who, when urged to witness a gladiatorial combat, at first steadfastly refused, even when bodily dragged to the arena. He closed his eyes in order not to see when suddenly there arose a great roar from the bloodthirsty mob as the kill was being made. Out of curiosity Alypius opened his eyes and gazed down at the scene of carnage below, then . . . "As soon as he beheld that blood, he drank

Christopher Lee in Taste the Blood of Dracula, *1969.*

down savageness, nor turned away, but fixed his eye, and drinking up the fury he became intoxicated with a delight in blood." After that Alypius not only became an enthusiastic spectator, but he went out of his way to encourage others to visit the arena and witness the bloodshed.

In spite of biblical prohibitions, moral aversions, or plain squeamishness, mankind throughout history has always somehow managed to maintain a preoccupation with blood. Whether it was a desire to witness carnage and bloodshed or the exact opposite, the connection has always been present. In both the Old and the New Testaments, blood has been characterized as having the power to wash away sins. In mythology and folklore there are numerous tales and legends concerning trees and plants that shed blood when cut or slashed. During times of great upheaval such as the French Revolution the multitudes fought for the privilege of witnessing the guillotine in action. In times of quiet there were never any problems in collecting crowds to observe public executions. From its very inception, the gory dramas of the Grand Guignol have drawn enthusiastic audiences from all over the world. Look at the immense popularity of the hardboiled

detective novel, rampant with sadism; the horror movie, the TV crime program; and such carryovers from ancient Rome as prize fighting, cock fighting, and bullfighting.

Though today we may shudder at the ancient Roman epileptic who drank gladiators' blood to cure himself, or at the physician who prescribed blood for scores of other ailments, we must nevertheless face the fact that such things exist today as well. The southern Slavs still drink the blood of weasels as an imagined cure for epilepsy. In olden times the compact written in blood was always more binding than the one drawn up in ordinary ink. Bonds of friendship are still occasionally formed by the cutting of arms and the intermingling of blood. In the days of the witch mania, love potions and charms frequently included blood as one of the most important ingredients. And many a church in Europe has among its sacred relics a silver vessel containing the clotted blood of a martyr saint. Yet on the other extreme we still have among us religious sects whose members would rather die than allow themselves to receive blood transfusions for fear of violating biblical injunctions.

From Bernhardt J. Hurwood, *Terror by Night*

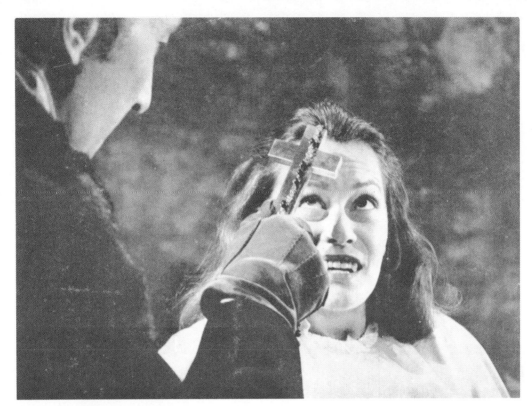

Peter Cushing menacing a female vampire in Hammer's 1958 Horror of Dracula, *the film in which Christopher Lee made his debut as the classic Transylvanian vampire count.*

MILLENIUM PRODUCTIONS
PRESENTS

GRAVE OF THE VAMPIRE

Grave of the Vampire *was originally made for television in 1974, and employed a very complex theme, which included not only vampirism but also the classic Oedipus myth. The vampire child, conceived during a rape, seeks to find and destroy his vampire father.*

Chapter 9

CINEMA AND THE IMAGE OF THE VAMPIRE

Certainly no medium has had a greater influence on the popular image of the vampire than motion pictures, and few other subjects have been treated in such a variety of ways. This is not intended as a detailed history of the vampire in cinema: there are many excellent books on the subject by film historians.

The first, and therefore one of the most important vampire films ever made, was Friedrich W. Murnau's *Nosferatu* in 1921. Although Bram Stoker's novel, *Dracula*, was still in copyright, Murnau did not bother with such minor details as acquiring the screen rights from Stoker's estate. Instead he retained the plot, made a few character changes, and switched the locale from England to Germany. The story, however, remained essentially the same. What was most significant about the film was the image of the vampire as conceived by the director and performed by actor Max Schreck, whose name, incidentally, is the German word for fear.

In *Nosferatu*, Count Dracula was called Count Orlock and, to quote from Donald F. Glut's *The Dracula Book:* "Schreck's Orlock remains as possibly the most hideous vampire ever to prowl the screen. His orbs seemed to burn from the blackened eye-sockets, which contrasted starkly with the pale face. The ears were pointed, as if belonging to some hellish demon rather than a being that was once a living man. The incisor teeth were elongated and sharp, and protruded from the front of the mouth. [Vampires have traditionally been described with the canines longer than the other teeth. The placement of Schreck's fangs in the front of his mouth suggested the teeth of some bizarre, human rabbit.] Schreck's hands had been made up with great, animal-like claws, which he extended like the talons of some monstrous vulture when advancing toward his victims. Schreck's Count Orlock was the *perfect* screen portrayal of a vampire."

A number of the traditional vampire characteristics were not attributed to

Schreck's Orlock. For example, he reflected in mirrors, he cast shadows, and he was unable to transform himself into a bat. Furthermore, his victims died from loss of blood but they did not become vampires themselves. The principal reason why this vampire was relatively uncomplicated, recognizable only by his strange, corpse-like appearance, was simply that in those early days cinematic special effects had not yet been developed to the fine mix of art and technology that they are today. Murnau's principal effects consisted of some double exposures, occasionally showing the vampire in negative image, and of slowing down the camera in order to produce the illusion that the count was capable of moving about with superhuman speed.

Murnau was also responsible for creating the impression that a vampire could be destroyed by sunlight. In Bram Stoker's *Dracula*, the vampire count was able to function in daylight if he so chose. As Glut says, "Murnau's reasoning that sunlight would somehow destroy a vampire was sensible. The vampire is a creature of the night which can be symbolically equated with evil. He is always defeated by some force of good—or of light. Sunlight was an ideal *deus ex machina* to enter and wipe out the fiend when his lust for blood became so great that he dared tempt the passing of his own element, the night."

Landmark film that it was, *Nosferatu* was not a commercial or critical success. The plot had been so obviously stolen from *Dracula* that a lawsuit charging infringement of copyright effectively relegated the film to a shelf in the vaults. Despite *Nosferatu's* relatively short public life, however, it succeeded in establishing a specific image of the vampire as an object of horror in the public mind.

German filmmaker Werner Herzog's remake of *Nosferatu*, which was released in 1979, was a stunning film that achieved results which were impossible in 1921. Filmed in sensuous dark colors, it had a moody musical score that enhanced the elements of eroticism absent in the original. Actor Klaus Kinski's makeup was virtually the same as Schreck's in the earlier version, but the personality of the vampire count was subtly different.

Since *Dracula* was in the public domain at the time Herzog made his film, he made certain changes that brought the new version closer to Stoker's novel. The vampire is called Count Dracula, and in the end Jonathan Harker, having suffered from the bite of the vampire, becomes an undead himself. It is the image projected by this Dracula that is especially intriguing. Though terrifying to look at, and certainly an object of loathing on the surface, he is multidimensional. Alone in his crumbling castle, his lust for blood is a compulsion that brings him no satisfaction. He is lonely, starved for the spark of humanity—for the soul he does not possess. When attracted to Harker's beautiful wife, Lucy, though on the surface he yearns for her blood, underlying his desire for it is what the director and cast project as human passion. In the scene where Lucy voluntarily surrenders to him in hopes of saving her husband, Dracula approaches her bed more like a lover than a predator, and before he falls upon her to suck her blood, in a gesture rife with irony, he gently raises her skirt and strokes her thigh as if he were a living man.

Despite the rats and plague he brought with him, this Dracula is as much an object to be pitied as his hapless victims.

In 1930, following the immense popularity of playwright Hamilton Deane's adapta-

Actor Klaus Kinski in the 1978 remake of Nosferatu, *a film which pays great tribute to the Murnau original. Director Herzog took such pains with the production that he went as far as to use many of the original locations and camera angles.*

Classic scene from the 1931 Dracula, *in which Bela Lugosi established the cinema vampire image which has yet to be surpassed.*

tion of *Dracula* for the Broadway stage, Universal Pictures successfully negotiated for the screen rights and formally announced its intention to produce the authorized cinematic *Dracula*. On the basis of a previous silent film, director Tod Browning chose Lon Chaney, Sr., for the title role. That earlier picture, *London After Midnight*, a 1927 MGM release, was not a vampire film *per se*. In it Chaney, portraying a London detective, disguised himself as a vampire in order to trap a hunted killer. Unfortunately Chaney died shortly before *Dracula* went into production and the search was on for a new leading man. Several actors were seriously considered for the starring role, including Paul Muni and Conrad Veidt. It soon occurred to Browning that the logical choice for the part would be the distinguished Hungarian actor Bela Lugosi, who had been playing *Dracula* to packed houses during the play's Broadway run. Thus the man destined to become the most celebrated of all Draculas donned his elegant cape and assumed the role that was to leave an indelible image in the public mind, one never to be eclipsed by another actor. The role also changed Lugosi's life. Not only did he become Dracula, he was permanently typecast, and though he retained his star status until his tragic death in 1956, when he was buried in his celebrated black cape, he was relegated for the rest of his career to parts in second-rate, low-budget horror films, all eminently forgettable. Indeed, the only reason many of them are still rerun on late-night television is that Lugosi still draws from beyond the grave.

A very significant aspect of the image created by Lugosi was the elegance he projected as the king of all vampires. He had no hideous fangs and never was he seen with blood and gore smeared on his lips, or staining his impeccable attire. He was never observed metamorphosing into a bat or ripping open a throat. The violence was implied.

Although there were a number of undistinguished vampire films made during the thirties, only one offered any serious departure from the familiar vampire image so successfully created by Lugosi—a Warner Brothers film called *The Return of Dr. X,* brought out in 1939, which belonged more to the science fiction deranged-scientist genre. The nontraditional vampire, played by Humphrey Bogart, was an executed doctor-murderer, brought back to life by a colleague of questionable morality. Bogart's vampire required a rare type of blood to survive. Though he was not portrayed as the classic undead, Bogart's Dr. Xavier was a gaunt, cadaverous, waxen-faced figure of a man with white-streaked hair and a sinister personality.

The popular Lugosi image of the vampire prevailed well into the 1940s. Other actors, notably John Carradine and Lon Chaney, Jr., gave the vampire different qualities, none of which ever quite succeeded. There was only one vampire and his name was Bela Lugosi. Chaney was not that good an actor. He was wooden and unconvincing. Carradine hammed up the part with an exaggerated style that audiences would not be quite ready to accept for another twenty years or more.

In 1948, Lugosi appeared again in a Universal Pictures spoof of vampires called *Abbott and Costello Meet Frankenstein.* Slapstick though the picture was, Lugosi gave the role its old panache by playing Dracula straight, and turned in a very creditable performance. Purists groaned at the thought of their indestructible vampire count in such company, but nevertheless the enterprise worked. When the picture was reviewed by the *Hollywood Reporter*, its critic said:

The idea of teaming Abbott and Costello with the stable of monsters that cavort at

Humphrey Bogart as a resuscitated corpse who requires a rare blood type in order to survive in The Return of Doctor X, *1938.*

U-I is one of those brainstorms that could be nothing less than hilarious in its completion. Happily *Abbott and Costello Meet Frankenstein* is just that—a crazy, giddy show that combines chills and laughs in one zany sequence after the other. There is something called a story involved, but it isn't important when Messrs. A and C begin clowning with the Wolf Man, Dracula, and Frankenstein's monster. . . . Abbott and Costello do their usual good job of building gags and keeping the laughs running constantly through the action. Their encounters with the monsters get the biggest giggles, naturally. Lon Chaney, as the Wolfman, and Bela Lugosi, playing his old role of Count Dracula, make excellent foils, as does Glenn Strange in the spot of the monster. . . .

A new era in cinematic vampirism was now dawning. Perhaps the rather civilized, fangless Dracula terrified relatively unsophisticated audiences of the thirties and to some extent those of the forties. Something stronger, however, was needed to shock and terrify audiences of the fifties who had lived through the real horrors of World War II and Korea.

As the 1950s unfolded, there was a veritable international eruption of vampire films. With the burgeoning of improved cinematic technology, producers tended to concentrate on elaborate, audiovisual special effects. With the exception of a few innovative filmmakers, most concentrated on producing stereotyped bloodsuckers spun off from the Dracula theme, few of which contributed anything new to the image of the vampire.

Certainly one of the most significant aspects of this growing interest in vampire cinema was its universality. Films on the subject were made in such diverse parts of the world as Malaya, France, Mexico, Italy, Spain, Japan, and Turkey. Meanwhile, the studios in Hollywood and England were busily creating new dark worlds. Although on the one hand the vampire image was reinforced by assorted carbon-copy Draculas, on the other a few new elements were beginning to creep into the genre.

A Turkish film, made in 1953, *Drakula Istanbulda*, or *Dracula in Istanbul*, incorporated elements of Bram Stoker and Vlad the Impaler. The vampire, a pallid-faced figure in a cape, was the first cinematic vampire to display fangs since the original Nosferatu. He was also unique because he did not display any aversion to crucifixes, but rather to the Koran.

Hollywood began the decade with great promise when Howard Hawks produced his science fiction thriller, *The Thing (From another World)*, in 1951. In many ways more terrifying than the traditional vampire, the Thing of the title was a giant, unspeaking, humanoid vegetable, an immense, bloodsucking carrot played by James Arness. It had arrived from outer space and was found frozen in a block of ice by a scientific-military mission.

With the Space Age just around the corner, and Wernher von Braun publicly declaring on the "Today" show that the technology existed to put men on the moon, Hollywood set about getting the jump on the scientists. Roger Corman started the trend of extraterrestrial vampires in 1957 with a horror-shocker called *Not of This Earth*. In 1958 a Döppelganger appeared called *It, The Terror from Beyond Space*, and still another variation on this theme appeared in a 1959 English film, *The First Man in Space*. Certainly the greatest departure was another Roger Corman film, made in 1959, called *The Attack of the Giant Leeches*.

The 1950s also produced the minatory teenager syndrome. In a climate that had brought such titles as *I Was a Teenage Werewolf* and *I Was a Teenage Frankenstein*, could the teenaged vampire be far behind? In 1957 American-International Pictures produced *Blood of Dracula*. The title was quite misleading for it had nothing to do with Dracula and even less with his blood. But it was a catchy phrase and virtually guaranteed to draw at the box office. The film deserves attention, however, because though it was little more than a potboiler designed primarily as one-half of a double bill on the drive-in circuit, it had one innovative ingredient.

The story was set not in Transylvania but in a girls' school located in a typical apple-pie American community looking suspiciously like Southern California. The vampire is Nancy, a neurotic young student, who gets involved with a chemistry instructor who obviously deserves to have her instructor's license lifted. Her interests extend far beyond the world of beakers, retorts, and test tubes. Among other things, she has in her possession a medallion which obviously once belonged to a vampire, perhaps even Dracula himself. The original owner apparently used it as a means of perpetuating the vampire species by magic. When teacher focuses the business end of a powerful spell on poor Nancy the child is transformed into a vampire.

Hideous to behold, she has an uneven widow's peak, coarse black hair, bushy wolfen eyebrows, pointed ears, a chalky complexion, and long pointed fangs. The heavy dark splotches under her eyes give her the appearance of having been on a monumental binge. Unlike the vampires of classic tradition this unfortunate teenage girl metamorphoses into a vampire periodically, sometimes by day, sometimes by night. Eventually, like Frankenstein's monster, she destroys the woman who turned her into an ugly bloodsucking beast. Not long afterward she loses her own life, naturally, by accidental impalement on a sharp piece of wood. Returning to her former pretty self as her life ebbs away she finds peace in reposeful death.

The year 1958 was a significant one in the realm of the cinematic vampire. In Great Britain a better than average production called *Blood of the Vampire* was released, starring the distinguished character actor Sir Donald Wolfit as Dr. Callistratus, a physician with a blood disorder, who engages in unlawful research among the hapless prisoners in a penitentiary hospital over which he presides. In the United States, United Artists released a passable low-budget film, *The Return of Dracula*, starring the popular Czech actor Francis Lederer. Though from the standpoint of personality, motivations, and goals, Lederer's Dracula followed traditional lines, in appearance he presented quite a different image. A handsome man with dark curly hair, Lederer wore conventional clothes, made no attempt to imitate Lugosi, and consequently presented a rather charming, continental image of his own.

The Return of Dracula was produced by Arthur Gardner and Jules Levy, who one year earlier had turned out another low-budget horror film with quite a different vampire theme—that of vampire-as-victim. Called *The Vampire*, and starring John Beal in the title role, the film dealt with the dilemma of a decent, dedicated physician who accidentally takes some so-called "vampire pills" produced experimentally by a colleague. He develops a Jekyll-and-Hyde personality, working to save lives by day but destroying them on those terrible nights when the vampire metamorphosis overwhelms him. Agonizing over his plight, unable to find a cure, he seeks release in death.

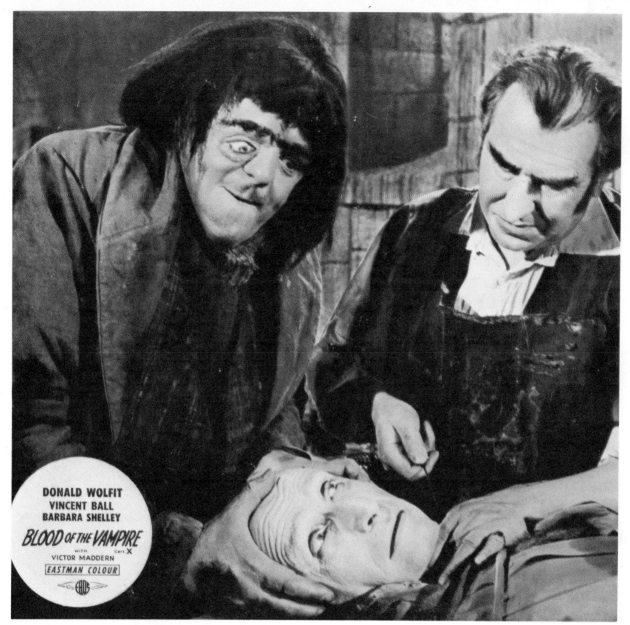

DONALD WOLFIT
VINCENT BALL
BARBARA SHELLEY

BLOOD OF THE VAMPIRE
WITH Cert. X
VICTOR MADDERN
EASTMAN COLOUR
EROS

Scene from the 1958 Universal/Eros production, Blood of the Vampire, *starring the late Sir Donald Wolfit (R).*

The landmark year of 1958 was also marked by Hammer Films' introduction of Christopher Lee in *The Horror of Dracula*, the first of their overwhelmingly successful Dracula cycle. In his succession to the title of Count Dracula, Lee almost singlehandedly laid to rest the old Lugosi image of the count, which had long since transformed itself in the public mind from horror to affectionate amusement. The handsome six-foot-four-inch actor gave Dracula a vigorous, energetic quality which implied supernatural strength, and he exuded an air of suave evil redolent with potential for bloody violence. He had sharp, pointed canine teeth and blazing red eyes. He was a walking paradox, at once repelling and terrifying, yet magnetically attractive. He had added a new dimension to the persona of Count Dracula. By projecting an element of eroticism, he embodied much of the actual vampire tradition and made his Dracula into the first true vampire sex-symbol. Discussing his approach to the role, Lee told interviewer Donald F. Glut, "I tried to remain true to the book. But otherwise it was entirely personal. What came onto the screen was a combination of my having read the book and trying to invest the character with his dignity and nobility, ferocity and sadness; also, my own personal interpretation of the character as I saw it from the script I was given."

Expert in providing the proper mix of sex and gore, Hammer saw to it that the Dracula films were amply decorated by beautiful, voluptuous young women wearing diaphanous low-cut gowns that permitted the camera to photograph ample cleavage at a moment's notice. Whenever they fell under Dracula's hypnotic spell, they were drawn to him in erotically charged trances. Often he would tantalize them until, with heaving bosoms, they offered him their throats in a manner akin to that of virgins eagerly surrendering their maidenheads.

But in addition to the erotic element which had always been implicit in vampire literature, Hammer went one step further. Aware of the fact that audience sensibilities were no longer as tender as they had been in the thirties and forties, executive producer Michael Carerras gave Hammer's creative team a free hand to follow their instincts. As a result they pulled out all the stops, and arrived at precisely the right formula of blood and eros, lush ominous settings, and baroque performances. Their cinematography was superb, and each Hammer film had the look of a picture budgeted at a much higher figure. What appeared at times like oceans of blood splashed against cinemascope screens to chill and delight audiences of all ages throughout the world.

The Horror of Dracula firmly established Lee as a horror film star of the first magnitude, but primarily because of his innate talent. Looking back over the vampire films he had done for Hammer, Lee commented on the first, "It's the only one that I've done that's ever been any good in my opinion. It's the only one that remotely resembles the original book." When *Horror of Dracula* was first released in the United States, *Variety* published an enthusiastic review:

There's gore aplenty in this import turned out by Michael Carerras' Hammer Films productions. Specializing in raw heads and bloody bones, Hammer also has to its credit last year's *Curse of Frankenstein*, which mopped up at the wicket. As was *Curse*, *Dracula* too is in color—a factor which tends to heighten the exploitation factor inherent in the film.

For those familiar with the original Dracula thriller, the Jimmy Sangster screenplay has ably preserved the

Advertising material for Jean Rollin's highly erotic 1969 French film, The Nude Vampire.

The 1970 Hammer/EMI production, Scars of Dracula, *explored the classic themes of good versus evil, light versus dark, human versus demonic.*

sanguinary aspects of the Bram Stoker novel. . . .

Both director Terrence Fisher as well as the cast have taken a serious approach to the macabre theme that adds up to lotsa action and suspense. Peter Cushing is impressive as the painstaking scientist-doctor who solves the mystery, Christopher Lee is thoroughly gruesome as Dracula, and Michael Gough is suitably skeptical as a bereaved relative who ultimately is persuaded to assist Cushing.

The Hammer Films productions made such an impact on the public that with the exception of nostalgia buffs who clung to the memory of their beloved Bela, a new vampire image in the likeness of Christopher Lee now became the accepted norm. Naturally, in a field which thrives on parrotry, imitators of the Hammer approach to vampirism began popping up like toadstools. In a few instances some of the shrewder ones even succeeded in casting Lee himself in the vampire role. Certainly one of the most unusual parts he played was that of Vlad Tepes himself in a documentary film made for television in Sweden. Called *In Search of Dracula*, it was based on the book by McNally and Florescu. Commenting on his appearance in the film, Lee later recalled, ''I went to Transylvania to do this documentary . . . '' and '' . . . appear in four different, if you like, guises. . . . One is the historical Dracula. . . . I look exactly like him. That may sound a bit difficult to believe, but it is, in fact, true. The resemblance is extraordinary. We found some of the paintings of the impaler in castles in Hungary and in the Tyrol and in the state museum in Budapest. And the resemblance is really ridiculous. It's almost the same face.''

Following Hammer's lead, especially where it involved the element of sex, a rash of erotic vampire films began to appear. The Italians, commencing in the fifties and going well into the sixties, produced a string of steamy potboilers involving everything from extraterrestrial aliens to well-endowed, panting *femme fatales*. There was even a muscleman epic, *Ercole Al Centro della Terra*, released in the United States as *Hercules in the Haunted World*. None other than Christopher Lee played Lyco, the vampire, here pitted against the demigod Hercules. Hoky though the idea sounds, it was made by the controversial director Mario Bava, who is a cult hero to devotees of cinematic arcana.

The 1960s brought a number of sexy females as vampires as well as victims. One of the best of these was a French-Italian coproduction titled *Et mourir de plasir*, written and directed by Roger Vadim, and starring his beautiful blonde wife Annette Vadim, Elsa Martinelli, and Mel Ferrer. It was based on the classic story by Joseph Sheridan Le Fanu, *Carmilla*, and the lovely brunette Martinelli played a role based on the vampire character in the original. As in the novella, there was a strong element of lesbianism. Beautifully photographed, the film had a hauntingly erotic quality that blended well with the inherent horror. A substantially emasculated version of the picture was released in the United States as *Blood and Roses*.

With the wide variety of vampires being brought to the screen from Cinecitta to Tokyo, the image, if it did not blur, certainly became a multiple one. The element of comedy appeared again. As early as 1959, the Italians made a film called *Tempi Duri Per I Vampiri*, or *Hard Times for the Vampires*; it starred our old friend Christopher Lee as Uncle Rinaldo, the vampire, and was released in the United States as *Uncle Was a Vampire*. Nothing was too extreme or too remote to involve vampires. A 1965 Italian-Yugoslav production called *La Sorella di Satana*, or

Barbara Steele, queen of the vampire pictures, in Revenge of the Vampire.

The Sister of Satan, dealt with the problems of a modern female vampire forced to deal with the Communists in contemporary Transylvania. Starring the striking, large-eyed brunette Barbara Steele as a vampire-witch who is revived after centuries in the grave, the film was released in the United States as *She-Beast* and in England as *Revenge of the Blood Beast*. Barbara Steele, with her lovely figure, dark hair, and luminous eyes is so haunting in her films that many consider her the most memorable female vampire to have appeared on the screen.

Blasted by the critics and cheered by kiddie audiences was the 1966 vampire-Western, *Billy the Kid Versus Dracula*. Essentially an old-fashioned Western with good guys and bad guys, Billy the Kid was sanitized to wear the white hat, and Dracula was hammed up in suitable cornball style by John Carradine.

Roman Polanski's 1967 film, *Le Bal de Vampires*, was released in the United States as *The Fearless Vampire Killers*, or *Pardon Me, but Your Teeth Are in My Neck*. This was a well-made, elaborate spoof of all vampire pictures, and ironically, marked the last film appearance of Sharon Tate, before she herself was the victim in an especially gory murder orgy.

It should come as no surprise that the most influential figure to capture the public fancy as the archetypal vampire of the 1960s came not from a motion picture but from television. It is very possible that the ABC-TV soap opera *Dark Shadows* was seen by more people before it went off the air in 1971 than all the vampire films previously made anywhere. Though the vampire-hero, Barnabas Collins, began the series as a menace, he eventually evolved into a tragic figure who loathed the fact that he was a vampire. At the other end of the spectrum, television produced still another vampire which, unlike the benign figure projected by Jonathan Frid's Barnabas Collins, was one of the most horrific figures of dread ever portrayed on the screen. This vampire appeared in an ultra-modern setting, amid the glitter of contemporary Las Vegas. The film was called *The Night Stalker*, starring Darren McGavin as a reporter who discovers the monster. What made this vampire so successfully terrifying was that he was rarely seen. In those fleeting shots where he appeared before the camera it was difficult to make out his features. He performed feats of such incredible strength that there was no doubt in the mind of the viewer that he possessed supernatural powers. The impression was reinforced by well-chosen shots of his victims after they had been attacked. The suspense was heightened and the drama intensified by the fact that only the reporter, Kolchak, was fully aware that the vicious killer stalking the streets was actually a vampire. The authorities in a world of jet aircraft, space travel, and atomic energy totally rejected the assertions of Kolchak, whom they regarded as demented and eventually hounded out of town. Thus, in the mind of the audience, who *knew* the truth, the vampire was somewhere out there waiting to strike again.

Actually, television had a great deal to do with a major shift in the vampire's public image. The tremendous need for material prompted writers to reach out for variations on old ideas as they never had before. They were forced to do this because of the basic lack of imagination on the part of most advertisers and network executives, who controlled program content. The vampire theme was ideal because it was "tried and true." There was an explosion of comedy and juvenile vampire spoofs. Vampires appeared in animated cartoons, on variety shows, and even in such unlikely series as *I Love Lucy*, *Crusader Rabbit*, *The Man From U.N.C.L.E.*, *Laugh-In*, *The Sonny and Cher Comedy Hour*, and *Get Smart*.

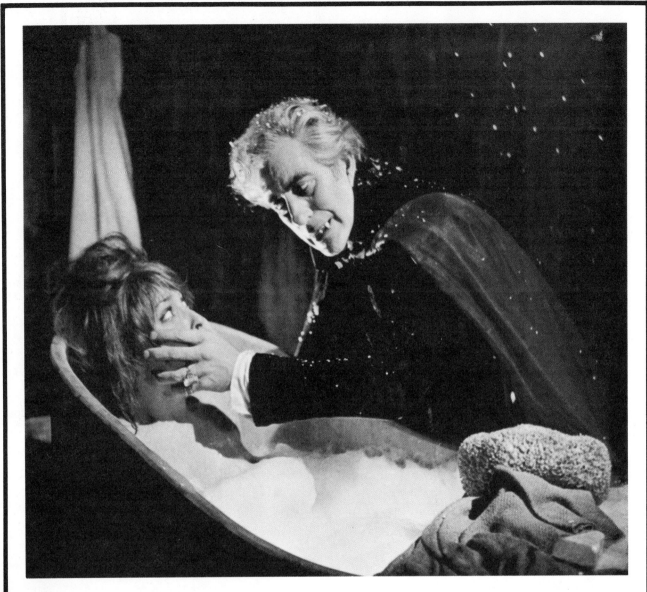

In Roman Polanski's 1967 Dance of the
Vampires, *Ferdy Mayne, as Count
Krolock, menaces Sharon Tate.*

With growing audience sophistication, mordant humor became more appealing. Unfortunately, on occasion, taste was abandoned completely. Certainly the nadir of tastelessness was *Blood of Dracula*, made in 1973 by Paul Morissey and Andy Warhol. Dracula was portrayed here by Udo Keir as an effete, youthful hypochondriac who could survive only on the blood of virgins. The complications arising from this situation—the scarcity of virgins in a Fellini-like Italy—resulted in excessive quantities of needless blood and gore that transcended horror and sank to the level of exploitational scatology. Also produced in 1973, in England, was a truly humorous vampire film called *Vampira*. It was charming, zany, and sophisticated, featuring as Dracula David Niven, complete with cape, fangs, and impeccable evening attire. The story dealt with a series of Dracula's adventures in London with bevies of beautiful girls, where he did everything from rescuing a young woman from a mugger to getting interviewed by *Playboy*. Never before or since did the image of the count acquire such a patina of elegance.

The old vampire theme was treated in a thoroughly original manner in a 1964 film made in Italy and starring Vincent Price. It was called *The Last Man on Earth* and dealt with what Barrie Pattison describes in *The Seal of Dracula* as "the lone survivor of an epidemic which has turned the world's population into vampires." The film was adapted from a Richard Matheson story, *I Am Legend*. In 1971 another version called *The Omega Man* was made in the United States and starred Charlton Heston and Rozalind Cash. Heston and Cash were the sole survivors besieged by hordes of hideous, zombie-like vampires who the audience knows will triumph in the end.

Shortly after the release of *The Last Man on Earth*, a young, highly innovative filmmaker from Pittsburgh, Pennsylvania named George Romero was very dissatisfied with what he saw. What happened is related by fellow filmmaker and teacher Roy Frumkes, who came to know Romero while making a documentary about the director's *Dawn of the Dead*.

Romero's films, *Night of the Living Dead* and *Dawn of the Dead* both spring from Matheson's vampirish novel [*I Am Legend*]. He didn't like either of the two films made previously from the book, and he didn't feel like dealing with the rights. Also, his approach moved it far enough away from the novel so that it wasn't plagarism. But *Night of the Living Dead* was his remake of *I Am Legend*, and it's better than the other two. It's genuinely scary. *Dawn of the Dead* continues it and a third one will complete the cycle. It will probably be called either *Dream of the Dead* or *Day of the Dead*.

Both of Romero's films mentioned here offer a sharply original image of the vampire not unlike that of the traditional Russian concept. Staggering across the screen are ghastly-looking, mindless corpses, ravenously hungry for the flesh of healthy humans who have not yet been infected by their terrible plague. Both *Night of the Living Dead*, which was shot in black-and-white, and *Dawn of the Dead*, which is in color, have become cult films among aficionados, and share the distinction of being controversial to the nth degree, having received both lavish praise and emotion-charged attacks.

Dawn of the Dead, filmed in a shopping center in Pittsburgh, employed some of the most grisly special effects ever to appear on the screen, effects that literally make the old Hammer "buckets of blood" look like Sunday school fare. Whether one likes or dislikes them is immaterial. From a professional standpoint one can only admire the artistry

In Columbia Pictures' Vampira, *David Niven portrayed the most suave and elegant Count Dracula ever to grace the screen.*

of special effects man Tom Savini, who skill-fully created everything from the slow dis-solution of those who succumb to vampirism to the lopping off of the top of a head by a whirling helicopter rotor.

Continuing his discussion of Romero's work, Frumkes said:

For me his best film is another, more direct vampire film, called *Martin*, which came out in 1977, and which I feel was one of the two best films of that year, the other being *Annie Hall*. This had all the qualities of *Annie Hall*, basically a tragic story with a humorous overlay and great ironies. Perhaps because it was so tragic and ironic it didn't find a market. It did fairly well on the midnight show circuit but that's about all.

The story deals with a neurotic, pos-sibly retarded young man who is possibly a vampire, we're never sure. Romero feels he is not. I felt he was. But the decision is definitely left up to the viewer. For ex-ample, he isn't strong enough to subdue women so he has to shoot them up with some sleeping drug in a syringe. He always hunts his victims hoping for romance and always is disappointed. His uncle is from the old world and believes him to be a vampire and constantly torments him about it.

It is really an unusual vampire film be-cause it totally demythifies the subject. One of the reasons I made a film about Romero's work is that I think he is one of the great stylists in America right now, and one who works independently. I had wanted to do a film about independent film making, so I approached Romero and asked if I could shoot my film on the set of *Dawn of the Dead*, which was just going into production. He had either heard of or seen my work, so he said, "Yes."

Frumkes's seventy-minute *Document of the Dead* not only offers valuable behind-the-scenes glimpses of how a horror film is made, it presents a panoramic view of Romero's previous works, which makes it of special interest to those with strong leanings toward the vampire genre. A nontheatrical film, *Document of the Dead* is distributed by Images Archives.

In some ways the vampire image will never change, assaults by sexploitationists, cornballs, and merchandising promoters notwithstanding. Serious actors like Louis Jourdan and Frank Langella continue to add dimension and freshness to their interpreta-tions of the vampire. Skillful comedy will always draw crowds. And the distinguished Shakespearean actor William Marshall's *Blackula* was an interesting departure from the routine lily white vampires.

Nothing proves the point more than the success of George Hamilton as Dracula in the film *Love at First Bite*. Discussing it with UPI reporter Frederick M. Winship, actor-producer Hamilton said, "It all started when I imitated an old Lenny Bruce Dracula routine for writer Bob Kaufman while we were vacationing in Mexico. We talked about doing a Dracula picture and after going on to another project we finally got around to it. I knew I wanted Kaufman to write the screen-play because we have a similar sense of humor."

Hamilton's Dracula is a sophisticated romantic who is evicted from his castle by Communist officials who have decided to convert the place into a training facility for gymnasts. He emigrates to New York and after a series of zany adventures with an equally zany collection of characters, Dracula woos and wins a slightly daft but glamorous model, turning her into a vam-pire, after which the two metamorphose into furry little bats and fly off into the moonlit sky.

Discussing his role, Hamilton said, "My Dracula character is based more on Bela Lugosi. . . . He had an inner fire and a fantasy that no one else who has done the role has caught. I saw Frank Langella in the current Broadway play and found it a mannered, stylized, tongue-in-cheek performance but I knew I had a more difficult task because our movie is a Mel Brooks type of comedy."

Hamilton's success was proven by the enthusiastic reception of *Love at First Bite* despite its deliberate poking of fun at virtually every ethnic group. Most took it in the goodnatured spirit that was intended except the Romanians, who took umbrage at one of Hamilton's lines, delivered as Dracula is leaving his castle permanently. Says he to a mob of pitchfork-, scythe-, and torch-bearing peasants reminiscent of early Lugosi films, "Just you wait and see, when I'm gone this place will be as lively as Bucharest on a Monday night!"

Certainly the most significant aspect of *Love at First Bite*'s success was Hamilton's skillful imitation of Lugosi's style, in which he maintained a delicate balance between outright mimicry and affectionate parody. If Hamilton's performance proved nothing else, it established beyond any doubt that of all the vampire images ever created, Bela Lugosi's is the most enduring.

American International Pictures' 1972 film, Blackula, *starring William Marshall, was the first vampire picture to capitalize on a burgeoning crop of black exploitation films. Despite some adverse reactions, it was in its own way something of a landmark.*

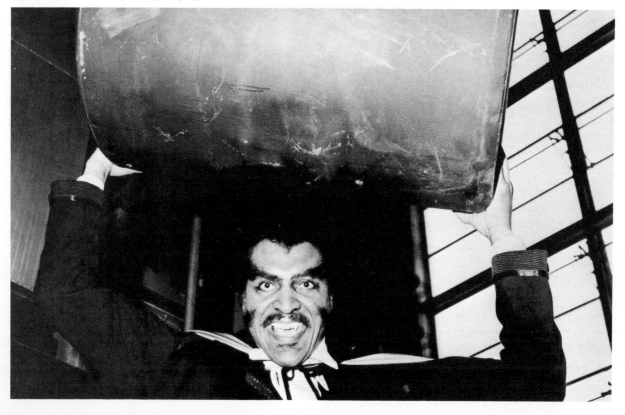

In the spoof Love at First Bite, *George Hamilton's Dracula awakens in a Harlem funeral parlor to the consternation of all parties concerned.*

Count Dracula

From **Dracula** By **Bram Stoker**

Christopher Lee in the 1969 Hammer production, Taste the Blood of Dracula.

Chapter 10

THE VAMPIRE IN LITERATURE

There are few subjects anywhere in the entire realm of literature which have sparked the imagination of novelists, poets, and playwrights to a greater extent than the vampire. The nature of the vampire being what it is has thus enabled skillful weavers of verbal tapestries to create spellbinding narratives that have manipulated, engulfed, and swept readers away into dark worlds comprising a tantalizing blend of eros, evil, pathos, and horror. What makes the literature of vampirism so fascinating is that its horizons are virtually limitless. So much has been written on the subject that there are serious collectors who have entire libraries devoted to this single subject.

Certainly the acknowledged masterpiece of the genre that overshadows all the others is Bram Stoker's *Dracula*, which began to chill its readers in 1897. The story of *Dracula* is so well known that it would be redundant to say more of the plot here than that it deals with the attempt by Count Dracula to establish himself in England, where it is his plan to increase and multiply his kind. Though he makes initial successful inroads, he is ultimately thwarted through the joint efforts of Dutch scientist-physician Abraham Van Helsing and English solicitor Jonathan Harker.

Though there was a long tradition of vampire fiction before *Dracula*, Stoker achieved what had only been approached by his predecessors. They may have shown us the mountaintop in the distance, but it was he who took us to the top and revealed what lay beyond. By endowing Dracula with every supernatural trait of tradition Stoker raised the count to a figure of towering stature who was the very incarnation of evil itself. But in addition to making Dracula the archetypal vampire, Stoker gave us a three-dimensional character who was noble, proud, and possessed of infinite self-confidence engendered by his knowledge of the power he had over ordinary mortals. Yet, in addition, ever present in his personality was the echo of former humanity. Dracula always gives us the hint that somewhere in the corridors of his intricate, dark mind there remains a spark of memory, a fleeting dream of what it was once like to live and love and enjoy the warmth of the sun.

Although there are long sections of *Dracula* that can become tedious to modern readers, when it comes down to sheer horror, Stoker's basic clarity of style has yet to be surpassed. With a skill that was developed out of necessity by Victorian writers, Stoker achieved another plateau of success in the way he depicted the erotic element inherent in vampirism.

The following excerpt is especially appropriate because it illustrates the point admirably. It is the scene in which Van Helsing leads his three friends, Harker, Dr. Seward, and Arthur Holmwood to the tomb of Lucy Westerna, Holmwood's deceased fiancee, who has become a vampire.

Never did tombs look so ghastly white; never did cypress or yew, or juniper seem the embodiment of funereal gloom; never did a tree or grass wave or rustle so ominously; never did bough creak so mysteriously; and never did the far-away howling of dogs send such a woeful presage through the night. . . . We saw a white figure advance—a dim white figure, which held something dark at its breast. The figure stopped, and at the moment a ray of moonlight fell upon the masses of driving clouds and showed in startling prominence a dark haired woman dressed in the cerements of the grave. We could not see the face, it was bent down over what we saw to be a fair haired child. . . . My own heart grew cold as ice, and I could hear the gasp of Arthur as we recognized the features of Lucy Westerna. But how she had changed. The sweetness was changed to adamantine, heartless cruelty, and the purity to voluptuous wantonness. Van Helsing stepped out, and obedient to his gesture, we all advanced too; the four of us ranged in a line before the door of the tomb. Van Helsing raised his lantern and drew the slide; by the concentrated light that fell on Lucy's face we could see that the lips were crimson with fresh blood, and the stream had trickled over her chin and stained the purity of her long death-robe.

. . . When Lucy—I call the thing that was before us Lucy because it bore her shape—saw us she drew back with an angry snarl, such as a cat gives when taken unawares; then her eyes ranged over us. Lucy's eyes in form and color, but Lucy's eyes unclean and full of hell-fire, instead of the pure, gentle orbs we knew. At that moment the remnant of my love passed into hate and loathing; had she then to be killed, I could have done it with savage delight. As she looked, her eyes blazed with unholy light, and her face became wreathed with a voluptuous smile. Oh, God, how it made me shudder to see it! With a careless motion, she flung to the ground, callous as a devil, the child that up to now she had clutched strenuously to her breast, growling over it as a dog growls over a bone. The child gave a sharp cry, and lay there moaning. There was a coldbloodedness in the act which wrung a groan from Arthur; when she advanced to him with outstretched arms and a wanton smile he fell back and hid his face in his hands.

She still advanced, however, and with a langorous, voluptuous grace, said: "Come to me Arthur. Leave these others and come to me. My arms are hungry for you. Come, and we can rest together. Come my husband. Come!"

Although the Marquis de Sade never wrote anything specifically on the vampire theme, in his celebrated novel, *Justine*, published originally in 1791, he offered a chilling insight to the mind of the human vampire. Some days after he has taken blood from a terrified young servant, the blood-

In the 1970 Hammer film, Vampire
Lovers, *Douglas Wilmer as Baron
Hartog prepares to punish vampire
Kirsten Betts.*

drinking Count de Gernande summons the girl and explains to her the bizarre relationship he has with his wife.

That woman belongs to me, Therese, she is my wife. And that title is doubtless the most baleful she could have, since it obliges her to render herself to the bizarre passion whereof you have been a recent victim; do not suppose it is vengeance that prompts me to treat her thus—scorn, or any sentiment of hostility or hatred; it is merely a question of passion. Nothing equals the pleasure I experience on shedding her blood—I go mad when it flows; I have never enjoyed this woman in any other fashion. Three years have gone by since I married her, and for three years she has been regularly exposed every four days to the treatment you have undergone. . . . My lust decreed her fate, it is immutable, she will go on in this fashion as long as she is able; while she lives she will want nothing and as I am incredibly fond of what can be drained from her living body, I will keep her alive as long as possible; when finally she can stand it no longer, well, tush, nature will take its course.

Despite the fact that *Dracula* is generally thought of as the seminal vampire novel, the truth is that he was beaten to the punch almost eighty years earlier by twenty-year-old John Polidori, personal physician and companion of Lord Byron. The novella, which today is all but forgotten except by scholars and vampire enthusiasts, was conceived during the "haunted summer" of 1816 when Percy and Mary Shelley were visiting Byron in his Swiss villa. One gloomy rainy day Byron suggested that each of the group write a ghost story, and all agreed. If Percy Bysshe Shelley actually produced anything for this unusual entertainment, it is not known. His wife, Mary, wrote her im-

mortal *Frankenstein*, and Byron outlined an idea for a tale of vampirism, but never wrote it. Polidori, however, envious of his companions' wealth, genius, and social status, picked up the theme abandoned by Byron and wrote *The Vampyre*. It was published in *The New Monthly Magazine* on April 1, 1819, under the erroneous byline of Lord Byron. When this long short story appeared, no one dreamed that it was to be a literary seedling destined to spawn a veritable forest of fiction and theatrical productions on the vampire theme.

The story opens in London at the height of the fashionable social season when "there appeared at the various parties of the leaders of the *ton* a nobleman, more remarkable for his singularities, than his rank. He gazed upon the mirth around him, as if he could not participate therein. Apparently, the light laughter of the fair only attracted his attention that he might by a look quell it, and throw fear into those breasts where thoughtlessness reigned. Those who felt this sensation of awe, could not explain whence it arose; some attributed it to the dead grey eye, which fixing upon the object's face, did not seem to penetrate, and at one glance to pierce through to the inward working of the heart; but fell upon the cheek with a leaden ray that weighed upon the skin it could not pass."

After being invited everywhere, the mysterious nobleman, Lord Ruthven, meets a wealthy young man named Aubrey. Aubrey and his young sister are orphans in possession of a large fortune, and the young Englishman is about to embark on an extended continental tour. When he mentions his travel plans to Lord Ruthven, who offers to join Aubrey, the younger man is flattered and immediately accepts.

As they travel about Europe Aubrey observes a number of disturbing peculiarities about his traveling companion. Ruthven gives lavish sums of money to undeserving denizens of the gutter, broken gamblers, thieves, and derelicts. Yet never does he ever offer a penny to the "virtuous poor." Aubrey soon discovers that recipients of Ruthven's largess are not as fortunate as they appear to be on the surface. The young Englishman "inevitably found that there was a curse upon it [Ruthven's money], for they all were either led to the scaffold or sunk to the lowest and most abject misery."

Eventually Aubrey and Ruthven arrive in Rome, at which time Aubrey becomes sickened by the older man's depravity. Thoroughly disillusioned by Ruthven and his lifestyle, Aubrey goes off to Greece by himself. In Athens he lodges with a family and soon falls in love with Ianthe, the daughter of his host.

As he travels around studying the ruins of ancient Greece surrounding Athens, Ianthe accompanies him and entertains him with tales of Greek legends and traditions.

Often as she told him the tale of the living vampyre, who had passed years amidst his friends, and dearest ties, forced every year by feeding upon the life of a lovely female to prolong his existence for the ensuing months, his blood would run cold, whilst he attempted to laugh her out of such idle and horrible fantasies; but Ianthe cited to him the names of old men, who had at last detected one living among themselves, after several of their relatives and children had been found marked with the stamp of the fiend's appetite; and when she found him so incredulous, she begged of him to believe her, for it had been remarked, that those who had dared to question their existence, always had some proof given, which obliged them, with grief and heartbreaking to confess it

was true. She detailed to him the traditional appearance of these monsters, and his horror was increased, by hearing a pretty accurate description of Lord Ruthven; he, however, still persisted in persuading her, that there could be no truth in her fears, tho at the same time he wondered at the many coincidences which had all tended to excite a belief in the supernatural power of Lord Ruthven.

One day Aubrey decides to visit a place some distance from the city, which requires him to pass through a wood, which his hosts insist is haunted by evils of an especially dangerous nature. They warn him that if he must indeed go there it is urgent for him to return home well before nightfall.

Though he intends to follow the advice, his journey back is hindered by a storm and he is forced to take shelter in a hut located in the heart of the haunted wood. "As he approached, the thunder for a moment silent, allowed him to hear the dreadful shrieks of a woman mingling with the stifling exultant mockery of a laugh, continued in one almost unbroken sound."

It is pitch black inside the hut. He finds himself grappling with an unseen individual who seems to possess supernatural strength against whom he is helpless. Unable to defend himself against his enemy, Aubrey is lifted bodily and hurled to the floor. The steely grip of cold hands tightens about his neck and he feels himself being strangled when unexpectedly his mysterious attacker loosens his grip, rises, and flees. A group of torch-bearing peasants arrive on the scene, at which time Aubrey discovers to his horror that there on the floor lies the lifeless body of his beloved Ianthe. Her neck and breast are smeared with fresh blood and on her torn throat are the teeth marks of the vampire.

Aubrey and the dead girl are taken back to her parents' house in Athens. The young Englishman languishes with a raging fever and the grief-stricken Greek couple die of broken hearts.

The dissolute Lord Ruthven unexpectedly arrives and nurses Aubrey back to health. The mysterious aristocrat takes such good care of the young man that he forgets their past differences and once again, after his recovery, continues his European grand tour with Ruthven. Not long afterward, in the wilds of the Greek mountains, the two men are attacked by bandits and Ruthven is fatally wounded. As he lies dying Ruthven says to his young friend, "Swear by all your soul reveres, by all your nature fears, swear that for a year and a day you will not impart your knowledge of my crimes or death to any living thing in any living way, whatever may happen, or whatever you may see."

Aubrey solemnly swears as Ruthven dies amid ghastly paroxisms of choking laughter. The dead nobleman's body is conveyed to a desolate mountaintop by the robbers, who have been bribed to comply with the dying man's last wish. None of them know that he is a vampire, for he is soon revived by the light of the full moon.

Aubrey returns to London only to discover that the vampire has returned in another identity, and is wooing his own sister, who in all innocence suspects nothing. Because of the solemn oath, Aubrey is helpless to tell what he knows and whenever he wavers in his resolve, often in the presence of the vampire, he is prevented from speaking by Ruthven's urgently whispered warning, "Remember your oath!" As the end of the year approaches Miss Aubrey's guardians announce her forthcoming marriage to "Earl Marsden," who is in reality the vampire. The hapless Aubrey is driven to the brink of madness and ruptures a blood vessel. It soon becomes apparent that he is dying. Desperately he tries to stop the impending nuptials, but he fails, and the tale ends on a somber note: "The guardians hastened to protect Miss Aubrey; but when they arrived it was too late. Lord Ruthven had disappeared, and Aubrey's sister had glutted the thirst of a vampyre!"

THE CREMATION OF A VAMPIRE

Early in the eighteenth century a well-known French botanist named Joseph Titton de Tournefort, who had traveled extensively in the Near East and Greece, wrote a fascinating account of his journey. One of the most bloodcurdling portions of his narrative was his eyewitness account of the burning of a suspected vampire by the peasants in a small village on the island of Mykonos. The following is a direct translation from his book Relation d'un Voyage de Levant, *published in Paris, 1917.*

"The man whose story we are going to relate was a peasant of Mykonos, in disposition naturally churlish and very quarrelsome, and this is a detail worth noting, for it often occurs in similar instances. This man then was murdered in some lonely country place, and nobody knew how or by whom. Two days after he had been buried in a small chapel in the town it began to be whispered abroad that he had been seen at night walking about with great hasty strides, that he went into houses, tumbled about all the furniture,

that he extinguished candles and lamps, that he suddenly fast gripped hold of people from behind, and wrought a thousand other mischiefs and knaveries.

"At first people merely laughed at the tale, but, when the graver and more respectable citizens began to complain of these assaults the affair became truly serious. The Greek priests candidly acknowledged the fact of these disturbances, and perhaps they had their own reasons for doing so. A number of masses were duly said, but in spite of it all the monster continued to carry out his trade and scarcely showed himself at all inclined to mend his ways no matter what they did. The leading citizens of the district and a number of priests and monks met together to discuss the business several times and in accordance with some ancient ritual of which I do not know the purport, they decided that they must wait for eight or nine days after the burial.

"On the next day, that is the tenth, a solemn mass was sung in the chapel where the body lay in order to expel the demon who, they believed, had taken possession of it. The body was exhumed after the mass, and presently everything was ready to tear out the heart according to custom. The town butcher, an old and clumsy fisted fellow, began by ripping open the belly instead of the breast: he groped a good while among the entrails without finding what he sought, and then at last somebody informed him that he must dissever the diaphragm. So the heart was finally extracted amid the wonder and applause of all who were present. But the carrion by now stank so foully they were obliged to burn a large quantity of frankincense when the hot fume comingled with the bad gases that were escaping from this putrid corpse but served to augment and extend the foeter which seemed to mount to the brains of those who were intent upon the loathe-

some spectacle. Their heated imaginations reeled, and the rank horror of the thing inflamed their minds with the wildest fantasies. Some even commenced to cry aloud that a thick cloud of smoke was being spewed out by the dead body, and in sober sooth amid the frenzy we did not dare to assert that this was merely the fume pouring from the censers.

"Throughout the whole chapel, and in the square which lies before it, one heard nothing but the cries of "vrykolakas," for this is the name that is given to those persons who return in this evil manner. The bawling and the noise spread through all the neighboring streets and the name was shouted so loudly that it seemed to cleave the very walls of the chapel itself. Many of the bystanders asserted that the blood of this poor wretch was a rich vermeil red in hue; whilst the butcher swore that the body was still warm as in life. Thereupon all mightily blamed the dead man for not really being dead, or rather for allowing his body to reanimated by the devil, for this is the true idea they have of a vrykolakas.

"As I have said, this name reechoed from every side in a most extraordinary manner. Large numbers of people went up and down through the crowd asserting that they could clearly see that the body was still supple and pliant with unstiffened limbs when they brought it from the fields to the church to bury it, and that obviously he was a most malignant vrykolakas. One could hear nothing but that word being repeated over and over again.

"I am very certain that if we had not ourselves been actually present these folk would have maintained that there was no stench of corruption, to such an extent were the poor people terrified and amazed and obsessed with the idea that dead men are able to return. *As for ourselves, we had carefully taken up a position near the body in order that we might observe what took place and we were retching and well nigh overcome by the stench of the rotting corpse. When we were asked what we thought about the dead man, we replied that we certainly believed he was indeed dead, but as we wished to soothe or at least not inflame their diseased imaginations, we tried to convince them that there is nothing extraordinary in what had taken place, that it was hardly surprising the butcher should have felt a degree of warmth, as he fumbled with his hands amid the decomposing viscera; that it is quite usual for noxious gases to escape from a dead body just as they do from an old dungheap that is stirred or moved; as for the bright red blood which still stained the butcher's hands and arms, twas but foul smelling clots of filth and gore!*

"But in spite of all our arguments and all our reasoning a little later on they burned the dead man's heart on the seashore, and yet in spite of this cremation he was even more aggressive, and caused more dire vexation and confusion than before. It was commonly reported that every night he beat folk sorely; he broke down doors and even the roofs of houses; he clattered at and burst in windows; he tore clothing to rags, he emptied all the jugs and bottles. Twas the most thirsty devil! I believe that he did not spare anyone except the consul at whose house we lodged. Albeit I have never seen anything more pitiful and more sad than the state of this island. All the people were scared out of their wits, and the wisest and best among them were just as terrorized as the rest. It was an epidemical disorder of the brain, as dangerous as a mania or sheer lunacy. Whole families left their houses and from the furthest suburbs of the town brought little tent-beds and pallets into the public square, in order to pass the night in the open. Each moment somebody was complaining of some fresh vexation or

assault; when night fell nothing was to be heard but cries and groans; the better sort of people withdrew into the country. . . . "

Tournefort goes on to describe how matters went from bad to worse. Any number of remedies were attempted to rid the community of this troublesome vampire. Masses were sung, solemn processions paraded the streets day and night, priests fasted, they even sprinkled holy water and washed the doors of all the houses on the street. At last they went as far as to pour a quantity of the precious liquid in the mouth of the corpse itself. Finally, says Tournefort, *"For our part, we kept impressing on the magistrates of the town that in such circumstances it was their duty as pious Christian folk to appoint a special watch all night in order to see what took place in the streets; and owing to this precaution at last they caught a number of other vagabonds who most certainly had been responsible for a good deal of the disorder and bother. This is not to say that they had originated it, or that they were even mainly to blame for the turmoil and disturbances. Yet they had some small part in the panic, and apparently these ruffians were released from prison a great deal too soon, for two days afterward in order to make up for the harsh fare which had been their lot whilst they were in gaol, they once more began to empty the jars of wine of those who were foolish enough to leave the houses empty and unguarded all night long without any sort of protection. Nevertheless the inhabitants placed their faith in prayers and religious observances.*

"One day as they were chanting certain litanies, after they had pierced with a large number of naked swords the grave of the dead body, which they used to exhume three or four times a day merely to satisfy any idle curiosity, an Albanian who happened to be visiting Mykonos just then took upon him-

self to say in a tone of the most absolute authority that in a case like this it was the last degree ridiculous to make use of the swords of Christians. 'Can you not see, poor blind buzzards that you are, that the handles of these swords, being made like a cross, prevent the devil from issuing from the body. Why do you not employ Ottoman scimitars?' The advice of this learned man had no effect at all; the vrykolakas was incorrigible, and all the inhabitants were thrown into the most consternation. They were at their wits' end to know what saint to invoke, when suddenly, just as if a cue had been given, they began to proclaim aloud throughout the whole town that the situation was intolerable; that the only way left was to burn the vrykolakas *whole and entire; and that after that was done let the devil possess the body if he could; that it was better to adopt these extremist measures than to have the island entirely deserted. For, indeed, already some important families had begun to pack their goods and chattels with the intention of definitely going to Syra and Tenor. The magistrates therefore gave orders that the* vrykolakas *be conveyed to the point of the island of St. George, where they had prepared a great pyre with pitch and tar, lest the wood, bone dry as it was, should not burn fast enough of its self. What remained of the carcass was then thrown into the flames and utterly consumed in a very few minutes. This took place on January 1st, 1701. We saw the blaze as we were sailing back from Demon, and it might justly be called a festive bonfire, and after this there were no more complaints about the* vrykolakas. *The people laughingly said to each other that the devil had been finally caught this time and they even composed a number of street songs and popular ballads mocking him and turning him into ridicule.''*

Tame though *The Vampyre* may seem to readers accustomed to such fare as *Rosemary's Baby*, *The Exorcist*, *I Am Legend*, and other tales of sophisticated horror that have gained such popularity in recent years, it was for its time the ultimate shocker. It was translated into French and German and spin-off versions were written by well-known authors like Dumas. Some adaptations were dramatized and played for a number of years to enthusiastic audiences. In 1828 in Leipzig, Germany, an opera called *Der Vampyr* was produced. Based on a French melodrama taken from the Polidori original with its locale switched to Scotland, *Der Vampyr* was relocated to Hungary. Spinoffs continued to be produced well into the late eighteen hundreds. Indeed, had poor Polidori been born a century later and been protected by international copyright laws, he would have died a very rich man.

By the year 1847 the fictional vampire had made great strides. In that year there appeared a novel, running about eight hundred pages, called *Varney the Vampire*, by Thomas Preskett Prest. It was a typical "penny dreadful" of Victorian gothic horror containing romance, mystery, and blood. The vampire-hero, Sir Francis Varney, alternately appeals to the readers' revulsion and hatred and compassion. In focusing his evil attentions on the unfortunate Bannerworth family, he sucks blood, kidnaps, and heaps vituperations on them. Not only that, he endeavors to take their family home away from them. At other times he elicits the reader's sympathy, especially when an angry mob sets out to lynch him. As the novel progresses he tries to redeem himself. We learn that he would be much happier if he were not a vampire, but is driven by forces beyond his control. Eventually he flees to Italy and commits suicide by flinging himself into the mouth of Vesuvius. A lurid novel, filled with purple prose, *Varney the Vampire* could hardly be regarded today as anything more than a literary curiosity.

A short story by Theophile Gautier which appeared in Paris in 1836 is as gripping and poignant a human drama as it was when it first came out. Published as *La Morte Amoureuse*, it has been published in English under such titles as *The Dead Leman* and *Clarimonde*. It is a delicate tale of erotic decadence reminiscent of Baudelaire. The story deals with the obsession of an innocent young country priest, Romuald, with a beautiful vampire, who in life had been a courtesan. She is described by Gautier:

> That woman was an angel or a demon, perhaps both; she certainly did not issue from the loins of Eve our common mother. Teeth of the purest pearl sparkled in her ruddy smile, and little dimples appeared with each motion of her mouth in the satiny rose of her adorable cheeks. As for her nostrils, they were regal in their graceful and dignified shape, and indicated the noblest origin. A luster as of agate played on the smooth, glossy skin of her half-bare shoulders and strings of great blond pearls, of a shade almost like her neck, hung down upon her bosom. From time to time she elevated her head with the undulating grace of a snake, or of a startled peacock, and imparted a slight quiver to the high embroidered openwork ruff which surrounded her neck like a silver trellis work.

Romuald's obsession becomes so all-encompassing that before long he finds himself transported in some mysterious way to a glittering world in which Clarimonde is his mistress. Before long the tortured priest is no longer sure of his own identity, and he cries out, "Sometimes I thought I was a priest, who dreamed every night he was a nobleman, sometimes that I was a nobleman who dreamed that he was a priest. I could no longer distinguish dreams from real life; I did not know where reality began and illusion ended. The dissolute, supercilious young lord jeered at the priest, and the priest abhorred the dissipations of the young lord."

But whether he was the dissolute young lord or the young bucolic priest, his love for the perverse Clarimonde remained the same. Eventually Abbé Serapion orders young Romuald to accompany him to a deserted cemetery, where they seek and find the tomb of Clarimonde. Then, after exhuming her body the abbé sprinkles it with holy water, rendering it into dust. The spell of the vampire is broken. The arrogant young lord recedes to the shadowy dream world from whence he came, and all that remains is the poor, humble priest, alone with memories he dares not revive.

In 1872 a short novel called *Carmilla* was published by the Irish novelist Joseph Sheridan Le Fanu in a collection entitled *In a Glass Darkly*. Le Fanu was one of the ablest practitioners of gothic horror, and *Carmilla* stands alongside of *Dracula* as a landmark work of vampire fiction. What *Dracula* did for the male vampire, *Carmilla* did for the female.

The plot concerns a young woman named Laura, who lives in an isolated castle in Styria, a province of southeast Austria. The atmosphere of the place is one of brooding darkness, the tone of which Le Fanu skillfully maintains throughout. The nearest village is half-deserted, and in the grim shadow of Schloss von Karnstein, a ruined

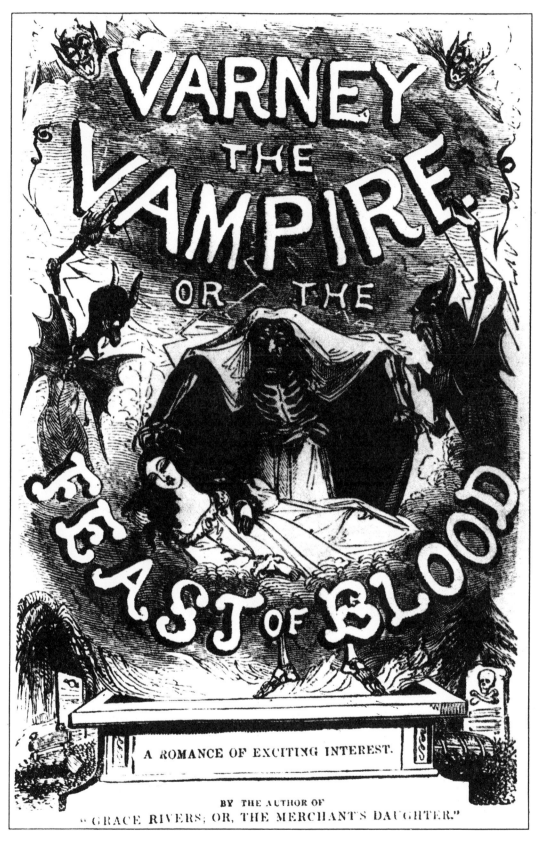

The cover of the 19th-century "penny dreadful" Varney the Vampire; or, The Feast of Blood, *by Thomas Preskett Prest.*

castle belonging to a family whose last member has been dead for over a century.

The narrative is from Laura's point of view, and opens with a brief setting of the scene, after which a beautiful, mysterious stranger named Carmilla comes to stay as a result of an accident to her carriage. She is pale and languid, in contrast to Laura's fair, energetic loveliness. Soon the two young women become passionate friends. Carmilla is secretive. She reveals nothing about her background or her past, which only tends to arouse Laura's interest. The relationship between the two is one of thinly veiled lesbianism, a subject too taboo to be discussed openly in Le Fanu's time. The following ex-

emplifies how well the author accomplished his purpose. Here Laura reminisces about her friend:

She used to place her pretty arms about my neck, draw me to her, and laying her cheek to mine, murmur with her lips near to my ear, "Dearest, your little heart is wounded; think me not cruel because I obey the irresistible law of my strengths and weaknesses; if your dear heart is wounded, my wild heart bleeds with yours. In the rapture of my enormous humiliation I live in your warm life, and you shall die—die, sweetly die—into mine. I cannot help it; as I draw near to you, you, in your turn, will drawn near to

Eventually Varney, pictured here satisfying his craving, tires of his "life of horror" and throws himself into a volcano.

others, and learn the rapture of that cruelty, which yet is love; so, for a while, seek to know no more of me and mine, but trust me with all your loving spirit."

And when she had spoken such a rhapsody, she would press me more closely to her trembling embrace, and her lips in soft kisses gently glow upon my cheek.

Carmilla is actually a vampire, dead for over a century and a half. Unlike the more familiar Dracula-type vampire, Carmilla is not a ferocious character. She is drawn to her victim by genuine affection and she does not appear to have her movements restricted to the night only.

The horrible truth eventually comes to light that Carmilla is none other than the long-dead Countess Mircalla Karnstein. Her tomb, long concealed in the crumbling ruins of the deserted Karnstein chapel, is discovered, and Laura describes what they find. "The features, though a hundred and fifty years had passed since her funeral, were tinted with the warmth of life. Her eyes were open; no cadaverous smell exhaled from the coffin. The two medical men, one officially present, the other on the part of the promoter of the inquiry, attested the marvellous fact, that there was a faint but appreciable respiration, and a corresponding action of the heart. The limbs were perfectly flexible, the flesh elastic; and the leaden coffin floated with blood, in which to a depth of seven inches, the body lay immersed. Here then, were all the admitted signs and proofs of vampirism."

The vampire, of course, is destroyed in the traditional manner and the story of Carmilla concludes. In a fascinating epilogue, Le Fanu provides further comment about vampires, synthesized no doubt from his own researches on the subject:

The vampire is prone to be fascinated by an engrossing vehemence, resembling the passion of love, by particular persons. In pursuit of these it will exercise inexhaustable patience and strategem, for access to a particular object may be obstructed in a hundred ways. It will never desist until it has satiated its passion, and drains the very life of its coveted victim. But it will, in these cases, husband and protract its murderous enjoyment with the refinement of an epicure, and heighten it by the gradual approaches of an artful courtship. In these cases it seems to yearn for something like sympathy and consent. In ordinary ones it goes direct to its object, overpowers with violence, and strangles and exhausts often at a single feast.

No discussion of the vampire in literature would be complete without at least a passing mention of Goethe's *The Bride of Corinth*. Based directly on the story of Phlegon of Tralles, it tells of a dead young woman who returns from her grave to rendezvous with her living lover. In a similar vein is another German work by a contemporary of Goethe's named Gottfried August Bürger. Written in the style of a folk ballad, it is a macabre tale, titled *Lenore*, which may have influenced Edgar Allan Poe. The story line is a simple one, telling of a dead soldier who returns from the grave to carry off his sweetheart on horseback. Returning to the cemetery he summons a weird assortment of spirits and together they celebrate an unearthly wedding between the living woman and her corpse-sweetheart.

One of the more lurid allusions to a vampire appears in the epic poem, *Thalaba the Destroyer*, by Robert Southey, who was poet laureate of England. Composed between July 1799 and July 1800, it was published one year later. Though popular in its day, it has fallen into a well-deserved eclipse. But as an oddity a short excerpt is worth a brief look.

> A night of darkness and of storm!
> Into the chamber of the tomb
> Thalaba led the old man,
> To roof him from the rain.
> A night of storms! The wind
> Swept through the moonless sky,
> And moan'd among the pillar'd
>   sephulchres;
> And in the pauses of its sweep
> They heard the heavy rain
> Beat on the monument above.
> In silence on Oneiza's grave
> Her father and her husband sate
> The Cryer from the minaret
> Proclaim'd the midnight hour.
> "Now, now!" cried Thalaba;
> And o'er the chamber of the tomb

> There spread a lurid gleam,
> Like the reflection of a sulphur fire;
> And in that hideous light
> Oneiza stood before them. It was she . . .
> Her very lineaments . . . and such as
>   death
> Had changed them, livid cheeks and lips
>   of blue;
> But in her eye there dwelt
> Brightness more terrible
> Than all the loathesomeness of death.
> "Still art thou living, wretch?"
> In hollow tones she cried to Thalaba;
> "And must I nightly leave my grave
> To tell thee, still in vain,
> God hath abandoned thee?"

In contrast to Southey's turgid verse is another poetic description of vampirism, which appears in *The Giaour* by Lord Byron. Like *Thalaba*, *The Giaour* has a Middle East setting. The term giaour was one used by Muslims as a pejorative for those who abandoned their religious faith, especially Christians. In Byron's poem, Leilah, the beautiful concubine of Hassan the Caliph, runs off with a giaour to her ultimate doom. Later he takes holy orders and becomes a monk, then on his deathbed he tells his story. The curse which is described in Byron's lines relates to the belief, particularly in Greece, where he had spent a good deal of time, that vampirism was a punishment imposed after death for some dreadful crime committed during one's lifetime. Part of the punishment was the requirement that the deceased limit his vampiric attacks to those who were his loved ones while he lived.

But first on earth, as vampyre sent,
Thy corpse from its tomb be rent;
Then ghastly haunt thy native place,
And suck the blood of all thy race;
There from thy *daughter, sister, wife,*
At midnight drain the stream of life;
Yet loathe the banquet, which perforce
Must feed thy livid living corse,
Thy victims ere they yet expire,
Shall know the demon for their sire;
As cursing thee, thou cursing them,
Thy flowers are withered on the stem.
But one that for *thy crime* must fall,
The youngest, best beloved of all
Shall bless thee with a *father's* name—
That word shall wrap thy heart in
    flame;
Yet thou must end thy task and mark
Her cheek's last tinge—her eyes' last
    spark,
And the last glassy glance must view
Which freezes o'er its lifeless blue;
Then with unhallowed hand shall tear
The tresses of her yellow hair,
Of which, in life a lock when shorn—
Affection's fondest pledge was worn—
But now is borne away by thee
Memorial O thine agony!
Yet with thine own death blood shall drip
Thy gnashing tooth, and haggard lip;
Then stalking to thy sullen grave
Go—and with Ghouls and Afrits rave,
Till these in horror shrink away
From spectre more accursed than they.

Favored today more by novelists and short story writers, vampire poetry of any quality is a rare commodity. Here then, are two heretofore unpublished poems by an anonymous poet, who signs herself only by the initials A. T., and reproduced here for the first time through the courtesy of Dr. Jeanne Youngson, president and founder of the Count Dracula Fan Club.

Whitby

I walk the seasoned hills
Alone, displanted and bewitched.

I romp the dented cliffs
With eyes advancing on the sky

Alone with all I must not be
Of poison and of longing.

All that is of me unknown
Yet breathing.

I laugh at the winds
That blow past my caring

And run to the sea which holds
our laughter, and our undeath.

A.T. © Jeanne Youngson, 1980

No Longer Free

Since having come you chose to linger
    here
To churn the working of my inmost
    heart
And plumb the depths of my black-
    ened art,
You cannot move away and never hear
It matters not what distant course you
    chart.
What walls you build to keep us each
    apart,
Whether they be of silence, stone or
    fear.

You are no longer free, no longer whole,
For though you go your wide and
    separate way,
The fevered beating of our pulse is twin.
And when in the foreverness of soul
We shed this long remembered hurt and
    clay,
You'll see your anger die and love
    close in.

A.T. © Jeanne Youngson 1980

Although it has been very difficult for any novelist to surpass *Dracula* there have nonetheless been many attempts to perpetuate the vampire theme in horror fiction. Thanks to the proliferation of original paperback novels, a great deal of entertainment has appeared which, if lacking in all the qualifications for immortality, has certainly provided aficionados with many hours of pleasure. Paperback editors and publishers, for the most part being more willing to take chances than their hardcover colleagues, have consistently come up with a number of innovative novels. To their credit they have not shunned heretofore untouched themes, particularly humor and science fiction. Richard Matheson's *I Am Legend* is a prime example. One of the funniest vampire novels to appear during the paperback explosion of the 1960s was adapted from an unproduced screenplay by Mallory T. Knight, best known for his outrageously funny spy spoofs. This madcap venture into a formerly humorless genre was considerably ahead of its time, because thematically it closely resembles George Hamilton's *Love at First Bite*. Its title was *Dracutwig*, and it focused primarily on Dracula's daughter, an innocent young thing who was born as a result of the old vampire's seduction one night by the village nymphomaniac.

When the village girl's parents discover that she is pregnant they lead a mob of torch-bearing peasants to swarm Castle Dracula and force a shotgun marriage. After the ceremony is concluded the mother exclaims, "Just think, our daughter—a countess."

The mother of the child conveniently dies before the baby is baptized. At the christening the infant is mistaken for a vampire when she is frightened by a ray of sunlight reflecting from the priest's golden crucifix. She is then placed in a basket and returned to her father's doorstep with a note. Dracula happily takes her in and raises her with the intention of giving her the best of all worlds. The human servants care for her by day, his vampire entourage by night. The humans attend to her more prosaic needs, the vampires, because of their age and superior knowledge, to her education.

Young Dracutwig, so called because she is a twig on the old family tree, has as her sole playmate a pet wolf named Bela. Though somewhat pale and skinny, she is a pretty child, and otherwise quite normal. Untainted by vampirism because her father has threatened to stake any follower who dares violate the throat of his only child, she grows up delightfully unafraid of vampires. Yet she is totally tolerant of them. Unfortunately the temptation is too great for one of them and he does indeed nip her in the neck one night as she is seated before a mirror, which of course enables him to creep up on her without being seen.

She is so innocent, however, that she makes nothing of the incident. Meanwhile the time has come for her to go off to school. Dracula sends her to London to attend an exclusive girls' finishing school with a handful of credit cards and a heart full of youthful enthusiasm. She is ensconced in a posh London hotel and has at her disposal a Rolls Royce with chauffeur. And from this point on the action speeds up.

While breathlessly taking in the sights on her first night in London she inadvertantly happens upon the opening of a fashionable new disco. There she meets Harry Brockton, a wealthy fashion photographer, who, smitten by her exotic, pale slenderness, becomes her lover and soon makes Dracutwig the toast of London fashion circles. Together they have turned the "dead look" into an international sensation.

Scene from the off-Broadway production, The Passion of Dracula, *at the Cherry Lane Theatre, 1978.*

Harry just happens to be a hemophiliac, and his overprotective dowager mother disapproves of any girl who might snag him and his fortune. She becomes immediately suspicious of Dracutwig. But mama isn't Dracutwig's only problem. She is beginning to turn into a real vampire and as the change comes over her it wreaks havoc with her photogenic qualities. She begins to turn transparent and fuzzy on film. The old family dietary craving comes over her. But knowing about her sweetheart's hematic weakness she restrains herself in his case. Dracula *père* comes to call one night and discovers what has happened. There is little he can do but go home and punish the villain who disobeyed him.

Meanwhile, Mama Brockton, having gathered enough proof that Dracutwig is a vampire, attempts to kill the poor girl with a silver bullet made from melted-down family heirlooms. She does not know that "silver bullets is for werewolves." As a result of this serious error, mama is hauled off to a mental institution and declared incompetent. Dracutwig acquires a pink, satin-lined coffin, and a convenient tomb; her fickle erstwhile sweetheart takes control of the family fortune and marries another girl. Totally unaware of the vengeful streak that runs in the Dracula family bloodline, he is similarly unaware, as he drives off on his honeymoon, that a medium-sized bat with glittering eyes and sharp teeth is flapping its wings and drawing closer to his limousine. And so ends *Dracutwig*.

It is unfortunate that the humor in *Dracutwig* was so far ahead of its time. It failed to click either as a screen play or as a novel.

A series of novels featuring the further adventures of Dracula gained a slight degree of popularity in the early 1970s, as did a number of novelizations based on the television series *Dark Shadows*. Similarly popular were the *Vampirella* novels. The first serious novel to present an alternative viewpoint of vampirism was *Interview with the Vampire*, by Anne Rice. It was the first time the vampire told his own story in very sympathetic terms. Stephen King's *Salem's Lot*, a chilling novel of vampirism in a small New England town, enjoyed a similar success. Interestingly enough, *Interview with the Vampire*, the more literary of the two, received most of the critical acclaim, while *Salem's Lot* sold more copies. A third novel, generically similar to *Interview with the Vampire*, my *By Blood Alone*, dealt with a vampire who, weary of his condition, seeks psychotherapy. The novel, placed in the framework of a whodunit, was well received.

It is in the short stories of science fiction and fantasy that we have seen the most original vampires. One of the most innovative was a 1955 story by Frederic Brown called *Blood*, concerning two 22nd-century vampires who flee from the world they know in a time machine, for the rest of their race has been destroyed in a bloody pogrom. They make vast jumps into the future, into times which they hope are remote enough that the word "vampire" will have been forgotten. All they yearn for is a place where they may survive and regenerate their kind. Each time they leap ahead they find that they are still remembered and feared, so they must continue to flee into a further future. At last they run out of fuel. Hungry and weary they encounter the new dominant race of earth creatures, telepaths, who no longer remember. The vampires are ecstatic, barely able to contain their relief and hunger. Then one of the telepaths says to them, "You also wonder about my origin and evolution. All life today is vegetable. I, a member of the dominant race, was once what you called a turnip."

Every lover of every genre has his or her own favorite tale. In the realm of the vampire there are so many that it is difficult to make a choice. For those who like their horror mixed with romance there is F. Marion Crawford's *For the Blood Is the Life*, and for those who prefer their horror undiluted, shuddery and nameless, one need look no further than M. R. James's chilling tale, *Count Magnus*. And no doubt there are still others who prefer the exotic, and lean toward the strange stories of P'u Sung Ling's Chinese vampires, of voracious flesh-eating Arabian ghouls, and of wily Russian soldiers and peasants who are constantly outwitting their vampire enemies. But whatever one's preference be it traditional or avant-garde, the true aficionado knows that—like the vampire's need for blood—there will never be enough.

Frank Langella in the 1979 Universal remake of Dracula.

BIBLIOGRAPHY

Abbott, G.F. *Macedonian Folklore* (Cambridge, England, 1903).

Ascher, Eugene. *To Kill A Corpse* (London: World Distributors, 1965).

Aubin, Etienne. *Dracula and the Virgins of the Undead* (London: NEL, 1974).

Avallone, Michael. *One More Time* (New York: Popular Library, 1970).

Aylesworth, Thomas G. *Monsters From the Movies* (Philadelphia: Lippincott, 1972).

_____. *Vampires* (Reading, Mass.: Addison-Wesley, 1972).

Bloch, Robert. *Dragons and Nightmares* (New York: Belmont Books, 1972).

Brokaw, Kurt. *A Night in Transylvania: The Dracula Scrapbook* (New York: Grosset & Dunlap, 1976).

Brown, Carter. *So What Killed the Vampire?* (New York: Signet, 1966).

Burke, John. *Dracula: Prince of Darkness* (London: Pan Books, 1967).

Burton, Sir Richard. trans. *Vikram and the Vampire* (London: 1870).

Butler, Ivan. *Horror in the Cinema* (New York: International Film Guide Series, 1971).

Carden, Phillip. with Ken Mann, *Vampirism: A Sexual Study*, (San Diego: Late-Hour Library/ Phenix, 1969).

Carlisle, Robin. *Blood and Roses* (New York: Hillman, 1960).

Carr, John Dickson. *He Who Whispers* (New York: Bantam Books, 1957).

_____. *The Three Coffins* (New York: Dell, 1965).

Carter, Margaret L., ed. *The Curse of the Undead: Classic Tales of Vampires and Their Victims*, (New York: Fawcett, 1970).

_____. *Vampirism in Literature: Shadow of a Shade* (New York: Gordon Press, 1974).

Chetwynd-Hayes, Ronald. *The Monster Club* (London: NEL, 1976).

Clarens, Carlos. *Horror Movies: An Illustrated Survey* (London: Secker & Warburg, 1968).

Coffman, Virginia. *The Vampyre of Moura* (New York: Ace Books, 1970).

Cohen, Daniel. *A Natural History of Unnatural Things* (New York: McCall Publishing, 1971).

Conway, Moncure Daniel. *Demonology and Devil Lore* (New York: 1879).

Copper, Basil. *The Vampire in Legend, Fact and Art* (Secaucus, N.J.: Citadel Press, 1974).

Cramer, Robert. *Lugosi: The Man Behind the Cape* (Chicago: Henry Regnery, 1976).

Crowe, Catherine. *The Night Side of Nature* (London: 1850).

Daniels, Les. *The Black Castle* (New York: Scribners, 1978).

Dickie, James. *The Undead* (London: Spearman, 1971).

Douglas, Drake. *Horror!* (New York: Collier Books, 1969).

Dreadstone, Carl. *Dracula's Daughter* (New York: Berkley, 1977).

Eaves, A. Osborne. *Modern Vampirism* (Harrogate, England: Talisman, 1904).

Eisler, Robert. *Man Into Wolf* (London: Routledge & Kegan Paul, 1951).

Elwood, Roger. *Vampires, Werewolves and Other Monsters* (New York: Curtis, 1974).

Estleman, Laren D. *Sherlock Holmes vs. Dracula* (London: Penguin, 1979).

Falk, Lee. *The Vampires and the Witch* (New York: Avon, 1974).

Farson, Daniel. *The Man Who Wrote Dracula* (London: St. Martin's, 1976).

_____. *Vampires, Zombies and Monster Men* (New York: Doubleday, 1975).

Florescu, Radu and McNally, Raymond T. *Dracula: A Historical Biography of the Impaler* (New York: Hawthorne Books, 1973).

_____. *In Search of Dracula* (Galahad, N.Y.: New York Graphic Society, 1972).

_____. *The Essential Dracula* (New York: Mayflower Books, 1980).

Frank, Alan. *Monsters and Vampires* (London: Octopus, 1976).

Frazer, Sir James. G. *Fear of the Dead in Primitive Religion* (London: Macmillan, 1936).

Frederick, Otto. *Count Dracula's Canadian Affair* (New York: Pageant Press, 1960).

Garden, Nancy. *Vampires* (Philadelphia and New York: Lippincott, 1973).

Giles, Herbert A. *Strange Stories From a Chinese Studio* [trans. of the works of P'u Sung Ling] (New York: Dover, 1969).

Giurescu, Constantine *Transylvania in the History of the Romanian People* (Bucharest: Meridiane, 1968).

Glut, Donald F. *The Dracula Book* (Metuchen, N.J.: Scarecrow Press, 1975).

———. *True Vampires of History* (New York: HC Publishers, 1971).

Goulart, Ron. *Vampirella* Series (New York: Warner):
1. *Bloodstalk* (1975);
2. *On Alien Wings* (1975);
3. *Deadwalk* (1976);
4. *Blood Wedding* (1976);
5. *Deathgame* (1976);
6. *Shakegod* (1976).

Haining, Peter. *The Dracula Scrapbook,* (London: NEL, 1976).

———. *The Ghouls* (New York: Pocket Books, 1972).

Haining, Peter, ed. *The Midnight People* (New York: Popular Library, 1968).

Hall, Angus. *The Scars of Dracula* (New York: Beagle Books, 1971).

Hill, Douglas. *The History of Ghosts, Vampires & Werewolves* (Newton Square, Pa.: Harrowook Books, 1973).

Hughes, William. *Lust for a Vampire* (New York: Beagle Books, 1971).

Hurwood, Bernhardt J. *By Blood Alone* (New York: Charter, 1979).

———. *Casebook Exorcism & Possession* (New York: NAL, 1976).

———. *Monsters Galore* (New York: Fawcett, 1965).

———. *Monsters and Nightmares* (New York: Belmont Productions, 1967).

———. *Passport to the Supernatural* (New York: Taplinger, 1972; NAL reprint, 1973).

———. *The Vampire Papers* (New York: Pinnacle, 1976; orig. title: *Terror By Night* (New York: Lancer, 1963).

———. *Vampires, Werewolves, and Ghouls: The Enigma of Human Monsters* (New York: Ace Books, 1968).

———. *Vampires, Werewolves and Other Demons* (New York: Scholastic, 1972).

Jacobi, Carl. *Revelations In Black* (London: Panther, 1974).

Johnson, Ken. *Hounds of Dracula* (New York: Signet, 1977).

Jones, Ernest. *On the Nightmare* (New York: Grove Press, 1959).

Kaplan, Stephen. *In Pursuit of Premature Gods and Contemporary Vampires* (New York: Vampire Research Center, 1976).

Knight, Mallory T. *The Dark Shadows Book of Vampires and Werewolves* (New York: Paperback Library, 1970).

———. *Dracutwig* (New York: Award, 1969).

Lee, Christopher. *The Illustrated Dracula* (New York: Manor Books, 1955).

Lee, Stan. *Dracula Lives*, special edition (London: World, N.D.).

Lee, Tenith. *Sabella, or The Blood Stone* (New York: DAW, 1980).

LeFanu, Sheridan. *In A Glass Darkly* (London: 1872).

———. *The Vampire Lovers* (London: Fontana Books, 1970).

Linssen, John. *Tabitha fffoulkes* (New York: Arbor House, 1978).

Lory, Robert. *Challenge to Dracula* (New York: Pinnacle Books, 1973).

———. *Dracula's Brothers* (New York: Pinnacle Books, 1973).

———. *Dracula's Disciple* (New York: Pinnacle Books, 1975).

———. *Dracula's Gold* (London: NEL, 1975).

———. *Dracula Returns* (New York: Pinnacle Books, 1973).

———. *Drums of Dracula* (New York: Pinnacle Books, 1974).

———. *The Hand of Dracula* (London: NEL, 1974).

———. *The Witching of Dracula* (New York: Pinnacle Books, 1974).

Lovecraft, H.P. *Supernatural Horror in Literature* (New York: Doubleday, 1945).

Lovell, Mar. *An Enquiry Into the Existence of Vampires,* (New York: Doubleday, 1974).

Ludlum, Harry. *A Biography of Dracula: The Life of Bram Stoker* (London: Fireside Press/W. Foulsham, 1962).

McHargue, Georges. *Meet The Vampire* (New York: Lippincott, 1979).

McNally, Raymond T., ed. *A Clutch of Vampires* (New York: Warner, 1975).

MacCulloch, Canon John Abbot, ed. *The Mythology of All Races* (New York: Cooper Square Publishers, 1964).

MacKenzie, Andres. *Dracula Country* (London: Barker, 1977).

Manheim, Karl. *Vampires of Venus* (Manchester, England: PBS Ltd., 1972).

Master, Anthony. *The Natural History of the Vampire* (New York: Putnam, 1972; Berkley reprint, 1976).

Matheson, Richard. *I Am Legend* (London: Corgi, 1977).

Monette, Paul. *Nosferatu, The Vampyre* (New York: Avon, 1979).

Murphy, Michael J. *The Celluloid Vampire* (Ann Arbor, Michigan: Pierian Press, 1979).

Myers, Robert J. *The Virgin and the Vampire* (New York: Pocket Books, 1977).

Myring, Lynn. *Vampires, Werewolves and Demons* (London: Usborne Publishing, 1979).

O'Donnell, Elliott. *Werewolves* (London: Methuen, 1912).

Parry, Michael. *Countess Dracula* (New York: Beagle Books, 1971).

_____. *The Rivals of Dracula* (London: Corgi, 1977).

Pattison, Barrie. *The Seal of Dracula* (New York: Bounty Books, 1975).

Penrose, Valentine. *The Bloody Countess* (London: NEL, 1974).

Perkowski, Jan L., ed. *Vampires, Dwarves, and Witches Among the Ontario Kashubs* (Canadian Centre for Folk Culture Studies, 1972).

_____. *Vampires of the Slavs* (Cambridge, Mass.: Slavica Publishers, 1976).

Pirie, David. *The Vampire Cinema* (New York: Crescent Books, 1977).

Prest, Thomas Preskett. *Varney the Vampire, or The Feast of Blood* (New York: Arno Press, ND).

Quong, Rose. *Chinese Ghost and Love Stories* (New York: Pantheon, 1946).

Randolphe, Arabella. *The Vampire Tapes* (London: Futura Publications, 1978).

Reed, Donald. *The Vampire on the Screen* (Englewood, N.J.: Wagon and Star Publishers, 1965).

Rice, Ann. *Interview With the Vampire* (New York: Alfred A. Knopf, 1976; Ballantine reprint, 1977).

Rice, Jeff. *The Night Stalker,* orig. title: *The Kolchak Tapes* (New York: Pocket Books, 1973).

Robbins, Rossell Hope. *The Encyclopedia of Witchcraft and Demonology* (New York: Crown Publishers, 1973).

Romero, George. *Martin* (London: Futura Publications, 1977).

Ronay, Gabriel. *Exploding the Bloody Myths of Dracula and Vampires* (London: Gollancz, 1972).

_____. *The Truth About Dracula* (New York: Stein and Day, 1974).

Ronson, Mark. *Blood Thirst* (London: Hamlyn, 1979).

Rudorff, Raymond. *The Dracula Archives* (New York: Warner, 1975).

Saberhagen, Fred. *The Dracula Tape* (New York: Warner, 1975).

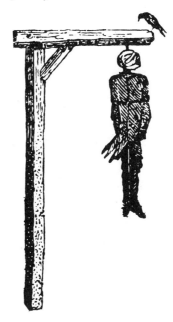

_____. *The Holmes-Dracula File* (New York: Ace Books, 1978).

_____. *An Old Friend of the Family* (New York: Ace Books, 1979).

Saxon, Peter. *Brother Blood* (New York: Belmont Books, 1970).

_____. *The Vampires of Finistere* (New York: Berkley, 1970).

_____. *Vampire Moon* (New York: Belmont Books, 1970).

Shedden-Ralston, W.R. *Russian Folk Tales* (London: 1873).

Shepard, Leslie, ed. *The Dracula Book of Great Vampire Stories* (New York: Jove, 1978).

Silver, Alain and Ursini, James. *The Vampire Film* (Cranbury, N.J.: A.S. Barnes, 1975).

Smith, Warren. *Strange Monsters and Madmen* (New York: Popular Library, 1969).

Stewart, Desmond. *The Vampire of Mons* (New York: Harper & Row, 1976).

Stoker, Bram. *Dracula* (London: 1897).

_____. *The Illustrated Dracula* (Chartwell, N.J.: 1975).

_____. *The Lady of the Shroud* (London: Rider and Company, ND).

Stuart, Sidney. *The Beast with the Red Hands* (New York: Popular Library, 1973).

Sturgeon, Theodore. *Some of Your Blood* (London: Sphere, 1967).

Summers, Montague. *The Vampire: His Kith and Kin* (New Hyde Park Park, N.Y.: University Books, 1960).

Tolstoy, Alexis. *Vampires: Stories of the Supernatural* (New York: Hawthorne, 1969).

Tremayne, Peter. *Bloodright: Memoirs of Mircea, Son to Dracula* (New York: Walker, 1977).

_____. *Dracula Unborn* (London: Corgi, 1977).

Trumbull, H. Clay. *The Blood Covenant: A Primitive Rite and Its Bearing on Scripture* (New York: Scribner's, 1885).

Underwood, Peter, ed. *The Vampire's Bedside Companion* (London: Coronet Books, 1976).

Usborne Guide to the Supernatural World (London: Usborne Publishing, 1979).

Vadim, Roger. *The Vampire* (London: Pan, 1978).

Volta, Ornella. *The Vampire* (trans. from the French by Raymond Rudorff) (New York: Award Books, 1962).

Volta, Ornella and Riva, Valeria. *The Vampire: An Anthology* (London: Neville Spearman, 1963).

Wagner, Margaret Seaton. *The Monster of Düsseldorf* (London: Faber & Faber, Ltd. 1932).

Wahl, Jan. *Dracula's Cat* (Englewood, N.J.: Prentice Hall, 1978).

Willoughby-Meade, G. *Chinese Ghouls and Goblins* (London: Frederick A. Stokes, 1926).

Wilson, Colin. *The Space Vampires* (London: Granada, 1977).

Wolf, Leonard. *The Annotated Dracula* (New York: Ballantine, 1976).

_____. *A Dream of Dracula* (Boston: Little, Brown, 1972; Popular Library reprint, 1977).

Yarbro, Chelsea Quinn. *Hotel Transylvania* (New York: St. Martin's Press, 1978).

Youngson, Jeanne, ed. *A Child's Garden of Vampires* (Chicago, Adams, 1980).

_____. *The Count Dracula Fan Club Book of Vampire Stories* (Chicago: Adams, 1980).

Youngson, Jeanne. *The Count Dracula Chicken Cook Book* (Chicago: Adams, 1980).

_____. *Count Dracula and the Unicorn* (Chicago: Adams, 1979).

_____. *Dracula Made Easy* (New York: Carlton, 1978).

_____. *The Further Perils of Dracula* (Chicago: Adams, 1979).

TEN THINGS YOU DIDN'T KNOW ABOUT VAMPIRES

1. Christopher Lee has played *Dracula* on the screen more than anyone else.
2. Vlad Tepes was afraid of vampires.
3. Bela Lugosi's *Dracula* was released on Valentine's Day, 1931.
4. White horses can detect the presence of vampires.
5. People who are born on Saturday will never become vampires, nor will they ever become their victims.
6. One can become a vampire by being born the seventh girl or the seventh boy in a row, to the same parents.
7. If a vampire is killed by a silver bullet, moonlight can revive him/her.
8. A vampire cannot leave his/her grave on a Saturday.
9. If a vampire gives the evil eye to a pregnant woman, her baby will be doomed . . . unless the spell is lifted by the church.
10. The easiest (but not absolutely foolproof) way to get rid of a vampire is to turn him/her over in his/her grave. When he/she starts digging, he/she may just dig through to China. Then it's *their* problem.

Bonus: Did you know that Julian Eltinge, London's famous impersonator, once had a skit in his repertoire called "Her Grace, the Vampire?"

*Rare production still from Universal
Pictures' original* Dracula, *courtesy of
Jeanne Youngson and the Count
Dracula Fan Club.*

FILMOGRAPHY

Since the year 1896 countless films have been made on the vampire theme. They have been produced in Argentina, Belgium, Brazil, Czechoslovakia, England, France, Germany, Holland, Italy, Japan, South Korea, Malaya, Mexico, the Philippines, Romania, Spain, Turkey, and Yugoslavia—just to mention those covered here.

To include every film ever made along with all the pertinent production information would require a volume in itself. Since this list is presented to give the reader a graphic example of how much has been done, and on how broad a scale, only the titles, countries of origin, and years of release are offered here. Serious cinema buffs and students who require more specific information should consult such works as the Library of Congress Motion Picture Catalogue of Copyright Entries; *The Vampire Film*, by Silver and Ursini, *The Seal of Dracula*, by Pattison; and *The Dracula Book*, by Glut, to mention only a few.

Abbott and Costello Meet Frankenstein	USA	1948
Andy Warhol's Dracula	USA/Italy	1974
Angeles y Querubines	Mexico	1972
Atom Age Vampire	Italy	1960
Attack of the Blind Dead	Spain	1973
Attack of the Giant Leeches	USA	1958
Bad Flower	South Korea	1961
Baron Blood	Italy	1972
The Bat People	USA	1973
Billy the Kid versus Dracula	USA	1966
Bite Me Darling	Germany	1970
The Black Harvest of Countess Dracula	Spain/Italy	1972
Black Sabbath	USA/France	1963
Black Sunday	Italy	1972
Blacula	USA	1972
Blood	USA	1973

Blood Bath	USA	1957
The Blood Beast Terror	England	1969
Blood Ceremony	Spain/Italy	1973
The Blood Demon	Germany	1967
The Blood Drinkers	Philippines	1966
Blood of Dracula	USA	1960
Blood of Dracula's Castle	USA	1969
Blood of Nostradamus	Mexico	1960
Blood of the Vampire	England	1958
Blood and Roses	France/Italy	1973
Blood Thirst	Philippines	1965
Blood of the Virgins	Mexico	1968
The Bloodless Vampire	USA/ Philippines	N.D.
The Bloody Fairy	Belgium	1968
The Bloody Vampire	Mexico	1962
The Body Beneath	England	1970
Bongo Wolf's Revenge	USA	1960
The Bowery Boys Meet the Monsters	USA	1954
The Brides of Dracula	England	1960
Bring Me the Vampire	Mexico	1965
Cake of Blood	Spain	1972
Captain Kronos—Vampire Killer	England	1973
Capulina versus the Vampires	Mexico	1972
Carry on Screaming	England	1966
Castle of Blood	Italy/France	1964
Castle of Lust	Germany	1968
The Castle of the Monsters	Mexico	1958
The Cave of the Living Dead	Germany/ Yugoslavia	1963
Chosen Survivors	USA	1973
Condemned to Live	USA	1935
Count Downe—Son of Dracula	England	1973
Count Dracula	Spain/Italy/ Germany	1971
Countess Dracula	England	1971
Count Erotica, Vampire	USA	1971

Count Yorga, Vampire	USA	1970		Dracula's Vampire Lust	Switzerland	1970
Creatures of the Pre-historic Planet	USA	1969		A Dream of Vampires	Brazil	1968
				Dugong Vampira	Philippines	1970
The Curse of the Karnsteins	Italy/Spain	1963		The Empire of Dracula	Mexico	1967
				First Man Into Space	England	1959
The Curse of Dark Shadows	USA	1960		Face of Marble	USA	1946
The Curse of Nostradamus	Mexico	1960		Evil of Dracula	Japan	1975
The Curse of the Undead	USA	1959		Forbidden Femininity	Italy	1963
The Curse of the Vampires	Philippines	1970		Frankenstein, the Vampire and Company	Mexico	1961
Dance of the Vampires (The Fearless Vampire Killers, or Pardon Me, But Your Teeth Are in My Neck)	England	1967		Frankenstein's Bloody Terror	Spain	1969
				Ganja and Hess	USA	1973
Daughters of Darkness	Belgium/ Germany/ France/ Spain	1970		Garu the Mad Monk	England	1970
				Genie of Darkness	Mexico	1960
				Guess What Happened to Count Dracula	USA	1971
Dawn of the Dead	USA	1979		The Great Love of Count Dracula	Spain	1973
Dead Men Walk	USA	1943		Goliath and the Vampires	Italy	1961
The Deathmaster	USA	1972		The Hand of Night	England	1965
The Devil Bat	USA	1940		Hannah: Queen of the Vampires	Italy	1970
Devil Bat's Daughter	USA	1946		The Haunted Castle	Japan	1971
The Devil's Commandment	Italy	1964		Hercules in the Haunted World	Italy	1961
Devils of Darkness	England	1965		The Horrible Sexy Vampire	Italy	1970
The Disciple of Death	England	1972		Horror of the Blood Monsters	USA	1970
Doctor Terror's Gallery of Horrors	USA	1967		Horror of Dracula	England	1958
Doctor Terror's House of Horrors	England	1964		The House on Bare Mountain	USA	1962
Dracula (Bela Lugosi)	USA	1931		The House of Dark Shadows	USA	1970
Dracula (Jack Palance)	USA	1974		The House of Dracula	USA	1975
Dracula (Frank Langella)	USA	1979		The House of Dracula's Daughter	USA	1973
Dracula, AD	England	1972		The House that Dripped Blood	England	1970
Dracula's Blood	Spain	1974				
Dracula's Daughter	USA	1936		The House of Frankenstein	USA	1944
Dracula's Daughter	Spain	1972		I Drink Your Blood	USA	1971
Dracula's Dog	England	1977		Incense for the Damned	England	1970
Dracula Has Risen from the Grave	England	1968		In Search of Dracula	Sweden	1971
Dracula in the House of Terrors	Germany/ Italy	1971		The Invasion of the Dead	Mexico	1972
				The Invasion of the Vampires	Mexico	1961
Dracula in Istanbul	Turkey	1953		The Island of the Dead	Italy	1966
Dracula Is Dead and Well and Living in London	England	1974		Island of the Doomed	Germany/ Spain	1966
Dracula's Lust for Blood	Japan	1971		Isle of the Dead	USA	1945
Dracula, Prince of Darkness	England	1965		It, the Terror from Beyond Space	USA	1958
Dracula, Prisoner of Dr. Frankenstein	Spain	1972		Jonathan	Germany	1970
Dracula Sucks	USA	1979		Kiss Me Quick	USA	1964
Dracula, the Dirty Old Man	USA	1960		The Kiss of the Vampire	England	1963
Dracula: The True Story	Romania	1979		Kuroneko	Japan	1968
Dracula versus Frankenstein	Spain	1969				

Dark Shadows *leading man, Jonathan Frid, before air time and (page 170) during the show.*

Kwaidan	Japan	1964		Queen of Blood	USA	1966
The Last Man on Earth	Italy	1964		The Queen of the Vampires	France	1968
The Legacy of Satan	USA	1973		Requiem for a Vampire	France	1971
The Legend of a Ghost	France	1970		The Return of the Blood Beast	Italy	1965
The Legend of Blood Castle	Italy/Spain	1972		The Return of Count Yorga	USA	1971
The Legend of the Seven Golden Vampires	England/ Hong Kong	1974		The Return of Dracula	USA	1958
The Lemon Grove Kids Meet the Monsters	USA	1966		The Return of Dr. X	USA	1938
The Lesbian Vampires	Germany/ Spain	1970		The Return of the Vampire	USA	1943
The Little Shop of Horrors	USA	1966		The Rider of the Skulls	Mexico	1967
Lips of Blood	France	1972		The Saga of the Draculas	Spain	1973
London After Midnight	USA	1927		Salem's Lot	USA	1979
Love At First Bite	USA	1979		Santo and the Blue Demon Against the Monsters	Mexico	1968
Love, Vampire Style	Germany	1963		Santo and the Blue Demon Against Dracula and the Wolf Man	Mexico	1972
The Lurking Vampire	Argentina	1971				
Lust for a Vampire	England	1946				
Mad Love of a Hot Vampire	USA	1971		Santo and the Vengeance of the Vampire Women	Mexico	1969
The Magic Christian	England	1962		Santo versus Baron Brakola	Mexico	1965
The Magician	France	1927				
Malenka the Vampire	Spain	1969		Santo versus the Vampire Women	Mexico	1962
Mark of the Vampire	USA	1935				
Martin	USA	1978		Satanic Rites of Dracula	England	1974
Men of Action Meet Women of Dracula	Philippines	1969		The Scars of Dracula	England	1970
				Scream Blacula, Scream	USA	1973
Midi Minuit	France	1970		Scream and Scream Again	England	1970
The Monster Demolisher	Mexico	1960		The Secrets of Dracula	Philippines	1964
Monster Go Home	USA	1966		Shudder of the Vampire	France	1970
My Son, the Vampire	England	1952		Slaughter of the Vampires	Italy	1962
Nocturna, Granddaughter of Dracula	USA	1979		The Snake Pit and the Pendulum	Germany	1967
The Norliss Tapes	USA	1973		Son of Dracula	USA	1943
North Star	USA	1933		Son of the Vampire	Malaya	1958
The Night Stalker	USA	1972		The Spider Woman Strikes Back	USA	1946
The Night Strangler	USA	1972				
Nosferatu, a Symphony of Horror	Germany	1922		Spooks Run Wild	USA	1941
				A Taste of Blood	USA	1967
Nosferatu, the Vampyre	Germany	1979		Taste the Blood of Dracula	England	1969
Not of This Earth	USA	1956		Terror in the Crypt	Spain/Italy	1971
Night of the Living Dead	USA	1968		Theater of Death	England	1966
O Macbro Dr. Scivano	Brazil	1971		The Thing (from Another World)	USA	1951
The Omega Man	USA	1971				
One More Time	England	1969		The Three Faces of Fear	Italy	1963
The Orgy of the Vampires	USA	1966		Throw Me to the Vampire	Mexico	1964
Oarlak, Hell of Frankenstein	Mexico	1961		Twins of Evil	England	1971
				Uncle Was a Vampire	Italy	1959
The Phantom of the Operetta	Argentina	1955		Valerie and the Week of Wonders	Czech- slovakia	1969
Plan Nine from Outer Space	USA	1956		Vaarwhel	Holland	1973
Planet of the Vampires	Italy/Spain	1965		Vampira	England	1973
The Playgirls and the Vampire	Italy	1960		Vampira 2000	Italy	1972
				Vault of Horror	England	1973

NOTE: There have been a great number of films produced around the world entitled The Vampire, Vampyre, or plurals of these. It would be pointless to list them all here.

A Vampire for Two	Spain	1965
The Vampire and the Ballerina	Italy	1960
The Vampire Bat	USA	1933
Vampire Circus	England	1972
The Vampire's Bite	USA	1972
The Vampire of Castle Frankenstein	Spain	1970
The Vampire Coffin	Mexico	1957
The Vampire's Curse	Malaya	1969
The Vampire Doll	Japan	1970
The Vampire of Düsseldorf	France/Italy/Spain	1964
The Vampire's Ghost	USA	1971
The Vampire Girls	Mexico	1967
The Vampire Happening	Germany	1971
The Vampire of the Highway	Spain	1969
Vampire Hookers	USA	1979
The Vampire Lovers	Italy	1961
The Vampire Man	Japan	1959
The Vampire of the Opera	Italy	1961
Vampire People	Philippines	1970
The Vampire Returns	Malaya	1963
The Vampire and Sex	Mexico	1969
The Velvet Vampire	USA	1971
The Voodoo Heartbeat	USA	1972
The Werewolf versus the Vampire Woman	Spain/Germany	1972
The World of the Vampires	Mexico	1960

Dracula attending to nefarious business in the crypt of his Transylvanian stronghold.

TEN BEST AND WORST OF LUGOSI

Best

1. *Dracula* — Universal, 1931
2. *Son of Frankenstein* — Universal, 1939
3. *The Raven* — Universal, 1935
4. *The Black Cat* — Universal, 1934
5. *White Zombie* — United Artists, 1932
6. *The Invisible Ray* — Universal, 1936
7. *Mark of the Vampire* — MGM, 1935
8. *The Ghost of Frankenstein* — Universal, 1942
9. *Island of Lost Souls* — Paramount, 1933
10. *Abbott & Costello Meet Frankenstein* — Universal, 1948

Worst

1. *Plan 9 from Outer Space* — Reynolds, 1959
2. *The Bride of the Monster* — Banner, 1955
3. *Glen or Glenda?* — Banner/Weiss, 1952/53
4. *Old Mother Riley Meets the Vampire* — Fernwood & Renown, 1952
5. *Zombies on Broadway* — RKO, 1945
6. *Bela Lugosi Meets a Brooklyn Gorilla* — Realart, 1952
7. *S.O.S. Coastguard* — Republic, 1937
8. *The Return of the Ape Man* — Monogram, 1944
9. *Scared to Death* — Golden Gate, 1947
10. *The Black Sleep* — Camden, 1956

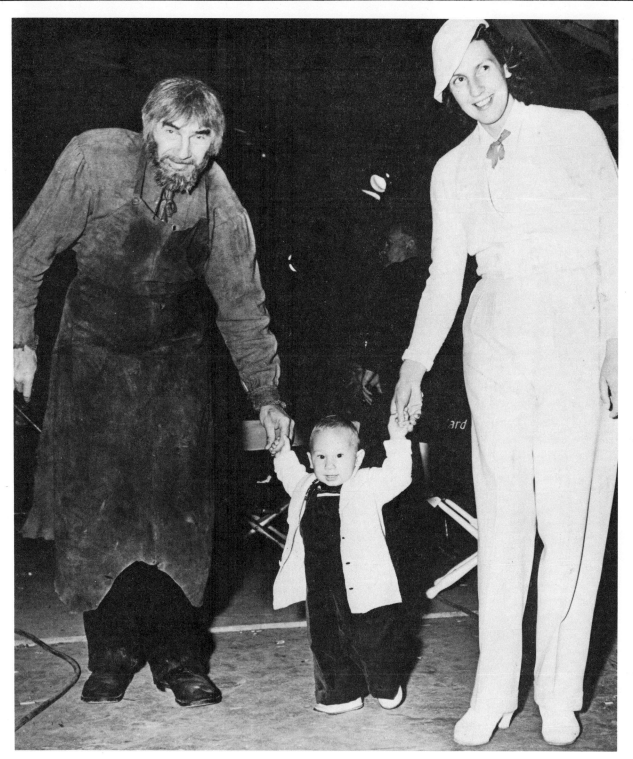

Bela Lugosi with his son, now a practic-ing attorney.

*L to R.: Ex-President Jimmy Carter
with Lita Dal Porto-Darwin, executive
vice-president, Count Dracula Fan Club,
California.*

176

VAMPIRE-RELATED ORGANIZATIONS AND PUBLICATIONS OF INTEREST

The Count Dracula Fan Club
29 Washington Square West
New York, N.Y. 10011
Dr. Jeanne Youngson, founder and president.

This is a light-hearted organization of individuals interested in vampiriana, werewolves, vampire films, and literature. Available to members are a book finding service, a newsletter, tee-shirts, greeting cards, and other memorable items, a number of which are available in a delightful "Dracpak." This club has an annual gala dinner every summer in London, England.

The Vampire Studies Society
P.O. Box 205
Oak Lawn, Ill. 60454
Martin V. Riccardo, director

The VSS is a serious organization devoted to the collection and dissemination of information pertaining to vampirism, lycanthropy, and other occult subjects and the psychology thereof. Their now-defunct publication, *The Journal of Vampirism*, contained a broad selection of articles on the above subjects.

The Vampire Information Exchange
c/o Fern S. Miller
P.O. Box 47
Hasbrouck Heights, N.J. 07604; or
c/o The Vampire Studies Society, above.
Dorothy Nixon, director

The VIE is a network of individuals seriously concerned with all aspects of vampirology. As the name of the organization implies, the object is to exchange information gleaned from any and all sources. The VIE periodically publishes a newsletter containing information supplied by members, as well as correspondence, names, and addresses of members, so that they may contact one another directly.

The Count Dracula Society
c/o Dr. Donald A. Reed, president
334 West 54th Street
Los Angeles, Cal. 90037

Devoted essentially to horror films and gothic literature, the CDS presents an annual Mrs. Ann Radcliffe Award.

The Dracula Society
Waterside Cottage
36 High Street
Upnor, Rochester, Kent NE2 4XG
England
Bernard Davies and Bruce Wrightman, cofounders

The society maintains a Dracula archive and is devoted to the memory of Bram Stoker and his magnum creation.

The Vampire Research Center
42-47 78th Street
Elmhurst, N.Y. 11373
Dr. Stephen Kaplan, director

The VRS is a serious organization concerned with research pertaining to real vampires.

The Count Dracula Society of Kentuckiana
P.O. Box 6816
Louisville, Ky.
Lewis Kelly, president

A potpourri of vampiriana in the headquarters of the Count Dracula Fan Club in New York, ranging from the Vlad Tepes souvenir doll once sold in Romania (top L) to edible examples of Dracula's commercialization. The doll in the top right photo is the Count on TV's Sesame Street.

The Christopher Lee International Club
18330 Jovan Street
Reseda, Cal. 91335
Pam Ellen Knox, president

Anomaly Research Bulletin
c/o David Fideler
303 East Fulton, Apt. 2
Grand Rapids, Mich. 49503

American Peter Cushing Club
131 East Joseph Street
Moonachie, N.J. 07076
Debbie del Vecchio, president

Children of the Night
Box 8187
Prairie Village, Kan. 66208

Compiled by Vincent Mattocks
© 1978, The Count Dracula Fan Club